UNSAFE
AT ANY
MARGIN

UNSAFE AT ANY MARGIN

INTERPRETING CONGRESSIONAL ELECTIONS

THOMAS E. MANN

American Enterprise Institute for Public Policy Research
Washington, D.C.

Thomas E. Mann is an assistant director of the American Political Science Association.

ISBN 0-8447-3322-9

AEI Studies 220

Library of Congress Catalog Card No. 78-20335

Printed in the United States of America

CONTENTS

ACKNOWLEDGMENTS

My indebtedness to others for help in bringing this book to publication is substantial. Richard Conlon, David Cooper, and numerous Democratic candidates for the U.S. House of Representatives made possible the congressional district surveys analyzed herein. Warren Miller, John Kingdon, Albert Cover, and Jerome Clubb, all of the University of Michigan, made valuable contributions to this work in its formative stage. Norman Ornstein, Howard Penniman, and Claudia Winkler each played an important role in its revision and publication. Finally, I am indebted to Evron Kirkpatrick and Sheilah Mann, without whom this book would never have been initiated, much less completed.

1
Introduction

The Traditional View of Congressional Elections

The major conclusion of the study reported in this book is that congressional elections are local, not national, events: in deciding how to cast their ballots, voters are primarily influenced not by the President, the national parties, or the state of the economy, but by the local candidates.

This thesis runs counter to the prevailing view, particularly of midterm congressional elections. In every midterm congressional election but one during the past hundred years, the President's party has lost seats in the House. Scholars have explained the loss as a reaction not to the performance of the government at the time of the elections, but to the outcome of the presidential contest two years earlier. Angus Campbell, in particular, developed a subtle theory of "surge and decline": in presidential years the winning party acquires an advantage in turnout and party preference that disappears in the subsequent midterm elections.[1] Members of the House elected on the strength of their party's presidential candidate are vulnerable when forced to stand for reelection alone.

In recent years many scholars have turned to the view long held by politicians and journalists that midterm elections are referendums on the performance of the President and especially on his handling of the economy. Edward Tufte in his *Political Control of the Economy* has developed a statistical model that accurately predicts the standardized vote loss of the President's party in any given midterm election from the yearly change in economic conditions and in presidential

---

[1] Angus Campbell, "Surge and Decline: A Study of Electoral Change," in *Elections and the Political Order*, Angus Campbell, Philip Converse, Warren Miller, and Donald Stokes, eds. (New York: John Wiley & Sons, Inc., 1966).

1

popularity.[2] Since according to Tufte the economy almost always performs less well in midterm than in presidential years, and since a President is more likely to be punished for bad times than rewarded for good, the President's party loses ground in midterm elections. The magnitude of this loss at the national level depends upon how badly the economy is doing and how unpopular the President is.

But this is only half the picture. How do changes in the national vote translate into changes in seats? From a national perspective, the rate at which votes translate into seats depends upon two factors: the number of districts that are marginal and the uniformity of the national vote change (or swing) across districts. So, for example, if the national swing in a midterm election is six percentage points in favor of the Democrats, the number of seats that shift to the Democratic party is a function of (1) the number of Republicans who carried their districts in the prior election by margins of less than six percentage points and (2) the extent to which the national swing of six percentage points is present in each of these marginal districts. (In fact, the national swing is never uniform across districts; evidence that strong national tides favoring one party are magnified in districts thought to be safe for the other party is presented in Chapter 4.)

This is where the famous and increasing "advantage of incumbency" comes into play. Traditionally over 90 percent of incumbents running for reelection win. Since the mid-1960s, their margin of victory has increased significantly and the number of seats falling in the marginal range has declined. First-term incumbents have done especially well—on the average over the last decade, five or six percentage points better than the national swing. Moreover, they have retained their advantage even in adverse years. In 1976 only two members of the post-Watergate Democratic class of 1974 lost their seats, although many of them had been elected in traditionally Republican districts.

The orthodox view, then, combining surge and decline, the referendum theory, and the increasing advantage of incumbency, would be that in 1978 we can expect the traditional loss of seats by the President's party to be partly offset by the insulation of incumbents from the ravages of national forces. As David Broder put it, "the 1978 election may give us the best test yet of the capacity of modern, publicity-conscious, service-oriented incumbents to beat the historical odds against their own political survival."[3] But is this the whole story?

---

[2] Edward Tufte, *Political Control of the Economy* (Princeton: Princeton University Press, 1978).

[3] David S. Broder, "November Mystery: Incumbents' Chances," *Washington Post*, June 18, 1978.

Reasons for Reassessing the Traditional View

The increase in the advantage of incumbency is a statistical fact; its meaning is less clear. Most observers see it as a cause for concern, a trend that is blunting the electoral instrument for change. Proposals for a constitutional limitation on the number of terms that a person may serve in the House or Senate have been revived, and the *Washington Post* has initiated a series of articles publicizing the electorally useful perks available to incumbents. An aura of suspicion surrounds congressional efforts to legislate changes in campaign finance practices and to increase the size of congressional staffs. Observers are becoming more and more sensitive to the disjuncture between individual accountability and collective responsibility, between the public posturing of members and their actions within the institution.

While I share some of this concern, the ills of the increasing advantage of incumbency are not as apparent to me as to others. During a period of supposed incumbent invulnerability and insulation, we find a Congress with high membership turnover (much of it due to the extraordinarily high number of retirements since 1972), major changes in internal structure and process, and a pervasive sense of electoral insecurity. It is only four years since the Republicans suffered a severe loss, and over the past decade a number of senior members have been defeated in primary and general elections. To my knowledge there simply is little evidence that incumbents have become less sensitive than they once were to strongly held policy views of the electorate.

One key to understanding how elections have managed to remain viable instruments for choice and change in the face of the increase in the advantage of incumbency is a shift that has occurred in the source of political stimuli in congressional elections. Two decades ago some analysts observed a growing nationalization of political forces in congressional elections, moving the United States closer to the British pattern of uniform swings across constituencies. Since they wrote, the opposite trend has set in. The forces for change in congressional elections, which had always had a strong local component, now originate even more at the district rather than the national level. Moreover, this shift has been accompanied by a widening separation of the presidential and the congressional votes. Where a party's presidential and congressional candidates once shared the same fate, they now go separate ways.

Increasingly, congressmen are responsible for their own margins of victory or defeat, and the electoral constraints they face are defined largely in their individual districts. National economic conditions and presidential popularity go far towards explaining aggregate national

3

change, but to the individual member concerned about his own vote, they are secondary. From his perspective, too, incumbency is a resource to be exploited more or less effectively, not an automatic advantage. Some incumbents, in the face of serious opposition, run well below their party's normal base of support. Others run far ahead. Incumbents and challengers alike realize that increasingly they alone, not their national party, are responsible for their success or failure.

If this is true, the 1978 House elections will be much more than a rearguard action within the Democratic party, in which the forces of incumbency attempt to withstand the rush of presidential unpopularity. Individual House members will be tested. How they fare will have implications well beyond the aggregate shift in the number of seats held by each party; these could include important changes in the distribution of power within the House, but also changes in the political profiles of individual districts and in the shape of particular congressional races in future elections. The nature of the test in each district will hinge on a number of factors: the normal political complexion of the district; the success of the incumbent in developing and maintaining both an attractive public image and the support of key individuals and interests within his constituency; the quality, financial backing, and skill of the challenger; the saliency of divisive local issues; the magnitude of negative feelings toward the Carter administration; and the extent to which the electorate associates the incumbent with its feelings about the President. What is most important for the voters, however, is the opportunity to choose between competing candidates.

This view of congressional elections has had little currency among political scientists. The reasons are not hard to find. In the past scholars have been struck by the public's abysmally low level of knowledge of congressional candidates and by the overwhelming tendency of voters to cast their ballots for the House according to their own party identification. What scholars have not found is an informed congressional electorate evaluating the candidates and choosing the preferred alternative. The notion of an uninformed electorate is not entirely alien to popular analysts either, who often base their judgments of a candidate's strength on simple "name identification" data—the number of voters who can recall or recognize his name. Indeed, one of the major advantages of incumbency is said to be the increased ability of members to get their names before the electorate.

But the fact is that we know relatively little about the amount of information voters bring to bear on their decision—or even whether they make serious judgments about congressional candidates at all. This study is an attempt to start finding out.

4

The DSG District Surveys

The research reported in this book grew out of my experience as a political consultant for the Democratic Study Group Campaign Fund during the 1974 and 1976 congressional elections. The DSG polling program was established in 1974 to provide Democratic challengers and marginal incumbents with an affordable means of gauging public opinion in their constituencies. Shortly after he took over as executive director of the Democratic Study Group in 1968, Richard Conlon began searching for ways of aiding his party's candidates while reducing the costs of congressional campaigning. His initial efforts included organizing campaign seminars, compiling committee and floor voting records of incumbent members, and developing prototype campaign brochures. In the spring of 1974 the two of us developed a system for conducting low-cost, volunteer based, telephone polling of congressional constituencies.

The key to the polling program was maintaining high professional standards in the design, execution, and analysis of the polls while substituting volunteer for paid interviewers. The experience in 1974, geared primarily to nonincumbents, was successful enough that in 1976 the DSG program was expanded and other organizations initiated similar efforts.

While these polls were designed to serve the immediate interests of politicians, I discovered that they could be mined for more dispassionate analyses of public opinion in congressional elections. To the best of my knowledge, congressional district surveys had never before been available for systematic scholarly research. Virtually all studies of congressional electorates have been based upon national surveys, which, because of their sample design and of the slim questionnaire content devoted to congressional races, are actually of very limited usefulness for this purpose.[4] The DSG polls provide an opportunity to address questions about levels of public awareness of congressional candidates and about the dynamics of change in public attitudes that have not been answered in the past.

A full description of the methods used in conducting the surveys is contained in the appendix. One methodological problem, however, should be addressed here, namely, the appropriateness of generalizing from a limited set of congressional districts, many of them marginal.

---

[4] There is one very encouraging development on this score, however. The University of Michigan's Center for Political Studies, which conducts the preeminent biennial national election study for the scholarly community, has redesigned its 1978 survey to meet the needs of those who study congressional elections.

The inferences in Chapters 3 and 5 are based largely on surveys conducted in forty districts, and the analysis of individual vote choice in Chapter 4 rests upon surveys in ten districts (although often two or three surveys were conducted in a single district). The question is: To what extent are the findings peculiar to marginal districts?

Clearly, the congressional districts with which I deal can in no sense be considered representative of all 435. A disproportionate number changed party hands as a result of the 1974 elections, moving in a period of four years from "safe Republican" to "safe Democratic." The vast majority of these districts moved into the marginal range in at least one of the two elections, although several remained solidly Republican or Democratic. While the special character of these districts must be kept in mind as the results are interpreted, there are several reasons for believing that the sample is not inordinately constraining.

First, since a number of genuinely safe seats are included in the sample, safe and marginal seats can be compared. It appears that the crucial difference between them in the level of public awareness of the candidates rests with the challenger, not the incumbent. Both the safe and the marginal incumbents in my sample were well known to the electorate. Challengers who oppose safe incumbents, on the other hand, often generate so little campaign activity that their candidacies go largely unnoticed by the public—which is one reason why the incumbents are safe. While the level of information about the challenger varies with the safeness of the seat, however, there is no reason to believe that the structure of the relationship between public opinion and electoral choice is fundamentally different in the two types of district.

Second, marginal districts, and especially districts that change party hands, are interesting in and of themselves. And even though the number of districts that fall in the marginal range in a single election has declined in recent years, the number that shift from one party to another over a period of years remains high.[5] Moreover, since we are interested in what elections mean for the way Congress behaves, it is important to note that safe incumbents learn from the experiences of colleagues in marginal seats, particularly from those who were once as safe as they.

---

[5] David Mayhew reports that "of House members serving in the [Ninety-third] Congress, 157 had originally succeeded members of the opposite party, 223 members of the same party, and 55 had originally taken newly created seats." *Congress: The Electoral Connection* (New Haven: Yale University Press, 1974), p. 34.

Summary

I begin in Chapter 2, then, by summarizing the intellectual history that forms the basis of our current understanding of voting in congressional elections. It is clear that the importance one attributes to public perceptions of congressional candidates (and more generally to forces that are within the candidates' control) depends largely on what one wishes to explain. If the question is what causes changes in the national two-party vote for the House, then one is safe bypassing individual congressional races and turning to national forces such as the performance of the President, the state of the economy, the length of presidential coattails in presidential years and their disappearance in midterm elections. While these national swings are usually relatively modest, they have clear political import, especially in midterm elections when they are the only national indication of the mood of the electorate.

If, on the other hand, one shifts the focus from change in the national vote to change in particular district votes—which, of course, is what most concerns the candidates—national forces become much less important. This is not to say that they are unimportant—the 1974 elections provide sufficient evidence that a strong national tide leaves its mark on most congressional districts. Yet the 1972–1974 national swing is itself a relatively poor indicator of the change in the vote in any given congressional district. In many districts the changes that occurred must be attributed to the candidates and the public's perception of them.

In Chapter 3, I tackle directly the question of what the public knows about congressional candidates. Here we see that while many voters are unable to recall the names of the candidates, the vast majority recognize the names when presented with them. The latter test is analogous to the situation the voter faces when casting his ballot, yet the former is almost always the standard by which "name identification" is measured. In addition, large numbers of voters have sufficient information to develop images of the candidates and to evaluate them on the basis of these images. The public responds to the political communication about the candidates that reaches its attention. The amount of communication is often constrained by the structure of the media market (candidates in major metropolitan areas can ill afford to buy television time, and they receive precious little free), by the inactivity of the challenger, and by the absence of clear differences between candidates that might generate public interest. Nonetheless, large numbers of voters have identifiable feelings toward the candidates, feelings that are not uniformly positive. To know a candidate is not necessarily to love him.

How important are these public perceptions of the candidates for the vote? In Chapter 4, I investigate this question by analyzing how candidate recall, recognition, and evaluation affect the voting decisions of individuals in ten congressional districts. (At this point the analysis becomes highly technical. Anyone who balks at models and tables may want to proceed directly to the last two sections of the chapter.) The vast preponderance of votes in congressional elections can be explained by public evaluations of the candidates. Party identification and simple name recognition are considerably less important than explicit candidate preference. Moreover, the number of voters motivated by assessments of presidential performance is extremely small. Incumbents do have an advantage over challengers—the public usually sees them as the more attractive alternative—but the size of that advantage varies with the incumbent's ability to attract favorable ratings from his constituents, and it does not necessarily prevent the challenger from becoming known and liked.

Increasingly, incumbents have at their disposal the resources with which to present themselves in a favorable light to their constituents, and challengers are usually hard-pressed to generate political communication sufficient to override this incumbent advantage. The difficulty for the challenger is finding both a basis for public dissatisfaction with the incumbent and the resources with which to make his case known to the public. Nonetheless, the potential for decisive changes in public attitudes during campaigns is certainly present. Several examples of such changes are presented at the end of the chapter.

In Chapter 5 the analytic focus shifts from the voting decisions of individuals to election outcomes in congressional districts. A comparison of the patterns of change in district returns between 1972–1976 and 1952–1960 reveals the fundamental shift in American electoral politics mentioned earlier: the forces for change in congressional elections increasingly originate at the district rather than the national level. Incumbents vary tremendously in their ability to run ahead of their party's normal strength. The extent to which election outcomes depart from the established political complexion of the district is largely a function of the visibility and attractiveness of the candidates.

I explore in Chapter 6 some of the implications of these findings about the congressional electorate for our representative system of government and speculate on future changes in congressional elections. The growing independence of House members from their party and from the President is one manifestation of the shifting locus of change in congressional elections. Whether it is improving the quality and the performance of the institution is uncertain.

In the long run, there is a fair prospect for increased competition in House elections, making them more similar to Senate and presidential elections. The decline in the importance of party identification and the increase in the visibility of the candidates make them more personally responsible and ultimately more vulnerable. Incumbents may have planted the seeds of their own destruction.

2
Determinants of Voting in Congressional Elections

The partisan division of the vote for presidential candidates during the last three decades has undergone volatile shifts. By contrast congressional elections appear very stable indeed. The national partisan swings between pairs of congressional elections have been only a fraction of those registered in presidential contests, and the Democrats have enjoyed uninterrupted control of the House of Representatives while frequently losing the White House to the minority party. In fact, the very modest deviations of the national vote for the House from the underlying partisan attachments of the electorate argue forcefully for the view that congressional elections elicit little public response beyond party-line voting. This conclusion is not seriously undermined when the focus of analysis moves from the national aggregate vote to the individual voter. Research has demonstrated that most voters have little information about the candidates beyond the party designation provided on the ballot and that the vast preponderance of ballots cast are consistent with the voter's party identification. The question then arises: Is voting in congressional elections so constrained by enduring partisan loyalties and massive public ignorance of the candidates that office seekers can scarcely influence the outcome?

The Stokes and Miller Thesis

The classic article "Party Government and the Saliency of Congress" published in 1962 by Donald Stokes and Warren Miller precipitated a lively discussion of this question among political scientists.[1] Stokes and Miller were engaged in an empirical examination of a major tenet of the "responsible parties" model of government, which holds that midterm

---

[1] Donald E. Stokes and Warren E. Miller, "Party Government and the Saliency of Congress," in *Elections and the Political Order*, pp. 194–211.

elections allow the public to pass judgment on the legislative record of the parties. The authors discovered that "what the public knows about the legislative records of the parties and of individual congressional candidates is a principal reason for the departure of American practice from an idealized conception of party government." Specifically, they found that while most votes cast for the House in 1958 were consistent with party identification (84 percent), there was very little programmatic or policy content in this electoral response. Moreover, what little deviation from party did occur was primarily a result of the public's awareness of the candidates, not of their judgment about the performance of the congressional parties.

The data presented by Stokes and Miller on the public's familiarity with the candidates were striking. Almost half of those who voted in the 1958 House elections claimed they had not read or heard anything about either candidate, though incumbents were visible to twice as many voters as were challengers. The perceptions of candidates that did exist were almost barren of policy content. However, public awareness of the candidates was related to party defection. The saliency of a candidate, defined by the authors as the extent to which the electorate claimed to have read or heard anything about him, was found to be critical for his ability to attract support from voters of the opposite party. This was true, the authors discovered, partly because, "in the main, recognition carries a positive valence; to be perceived at all is to be perceived favorably." When the few negative perceptions found in the interviews were taken into account, moreover, the relationship between saliency and defection was even more pronounced. Finally, the authors noted that candidate saliency is partly a function of common residence—the "friends and neighbors" factor.

This assessment of the responsible parties model soon led to the widespread acceptance of three propositions about congressional elections, each of which is a simplification of a more subtle argument made by Stokes and Miller: (1) Voting in congressional elections is primarily a ritualistic affirmation of partisan loyalty. The number of Independents and partisan defectors in the congressional electorate is exceedingly small and relatively inconsequential. (2) Current assessments of the performance of the national parties do not enter the midterm electorate's calculus of voting. Instead, national effects in midterm congressional elections result primarily from the receding of electoral tides washing in the prior presidential election. This "surge and decline" phenomenon minimizes the importance of the political forces operating at the time of the midterm election.[2] (3) The public is too poorly in-

---

[2] See Chapter 1, p. 1, including footnote 1.

formed to discriminate between candidates on the basis of their personal appeals or positions on issues; simple candidate saliency accounts for much of the partisan defection that does occur.

In recent years, there have been important extensions and revisions of these generalizations. With the benefit of hindsight, it is now clear that party-line voting reached a peak in 1958, just at the time Miller and Stokes made their study; the proportion of all votes for the House cast by party identifiers voting for their party declined throughout the sixties and settled to a level beneath 75 percent in the early 1970s (see Table 2-1).[3] Moreover, we know that partisan defections are far from inconsequential. Cover has demonstrated that in recent years they disproportionately favor incumbents.[4]

We also now realize that midterm congressional electorates are not entirely oblivious to the performance of the national parties. Kernell[5] working with individual-level data and Tufte[6] with aggregate data have both demonstrated that the public is inclined to punish a President for poor performance in office by voting against his party's congressional candidates in midterm elections. In addition, Arthur Miller and Richard Glass have shown that in 1974 the voters' assessments of the President's success or failure in dealing with economic problems were a key determinant of their vote for Congress, even more important than Watergate.[7]

Stokes and Miller were not unaware of this national influence on the vote for Congress. In *The American Voter* they (along with Angus

---

[3] Even this level of party-line voting might be inflated by the form of the question used in the Center for Political Studies (CPS) surveys. Respondents are asked, "Did you vote for a candidate for Congress?" (IF YES) "Who did you vote for?" "Which party is that?" Two potential sources of error are present, both favoring party-line voting. First, in the voting booth respondents are provided with the names of the candidates, in the interview they are not. Party defectors, unable to recall the name of the candidate, might mention their own party in the absence of the candidate stimulus. Second, respondents who mention voting for a candidate of one party and then incorrectly identify that candidate's party are coded with the incorrect party (which is most likely their own). As consequence of this coding procedure, defection was underreported by 1.6 percentage points in 1972. No systematic bias was present in the 1974 data.

[4] Albert D. Cover, "The Advantage of Incumbency in Congressional Elections," Ph.D. dissertation, Yale University, 1976, p. 53.

[5] Samuel Kernell, "Presidential Popularity and Negative Voting: An Alternative Explanation of the Midterm Congressional Decline of the President's Party," *American Political Science Review*, vol. 71, no. 1 (March 1977), pp. 44–66.

[6] Edward R. Tufte, "Determinants of the Outcomes of Midterm Congressional Elections," *American Political Science Review*, vol. 69 (September 1975), pp. 812–826, and *Political Control of the Economy*.

[7] Arthur H. Miller and Richard Glass, "Economic Dissatisfaction and Electoral Choice," unpublished manuscript, Center for Political Studies, University of Michigan.

Table 2-1
PARTY-LINE VOTING IN HOUSE ELECTIONS, 1956–1976
(in percentages)

Year	Party-Line Voters	Defectors	Independents	Total
1956	82	9	9	100
1958	84	11	5	100
1960	80	12	8	100
1962	83	12	5	100
1964	79	15	5	100
1966	76	16	8	100
1968	74	19	7	100
1970	76	16	8	100
1972	73	17	10	100
1974	74	18	8	100
1976	72	19	9	100

Note: Party-line voters are those who voted for the party with which they identified. (Those who considered themselves Independents but stated that they leaned toward the Democratic or Republican party are treated as party-line voters here and throughout the book.) Defectors are those who voted for the party other than that with which they identified. Independents are those who identified themselves as such and who voted for either candidate. Data may not add to 100 due to rounding.

Source: Data for the 1956–1970 period were taken from Robert B. Arseneau and Raymond E. Wolfinger, "Voting Behavior in Congressional Elections," paper presented at the Annual Meeting of the American Political Science Association, 1973, p. 10. The 1972, 1974, and 1976 figures were computed from data provided by the Inter-University Consortium for Political and Social Research.

Campbell and Philip Converse) document how evaluations of the Eisenhower administration's economic performance influenced the vote for Congress in 1958; they also state that "the party division of the vote is most likely to be changed by a negative public reaction to the record of the party in power."[8] Their point in "Party Government" was slightly different: that "the deviations that do result from national forces are not in the main produced by the parties' legislative records and that, in any case, the proportion of deviating votes that can be attributed to national politics is likely to be a small part of the total votes cast by persons deviating from party in a midterm year."[9]

---

[8] Angus Campbell, Philip E. Converse, Warren E. Miller, and Donald Stokes, *The American Voter* (New York: John Wiley & Sons, 1960), chap. 14 and p. 554.
[9] Stokes and Miller, "Party Government," p. 203.

The Problems of Saliency and Incumbency

What is seen in congressional elections is determined partly by the questions asked. In 1962, Stokes and Miller were looking for evidence that would bear directly on the responsible parties model; hence their emphasis on the content of the public's perception of the national parties' legislative records. A focus on national electoral *change*—a shift in the proportion of the national vote for the House captured by one of the parties in successive elections—directs attention explicitly to national forces of the kind that Tufte, Kernell, and others have been investigating. If the *distribution* of that national electoral change across congressional districts is of central interest, on the other hand, national forces are of little help. One of the distinguishing characteristics of congressional elections is the absence of a uniform swing; electoral forces whose origins are at the local district level insure a distinctly heterogeneous swing.[10]

The third generalization mentioned above—that the public's ignorance of congressional candidates forces them to rely on simple candidate saliency—has not been seriously challenged in recent discussions of congressional elections. For example, in 1976 Miller and Levitin observed that despite all efforts to supplement the generally inadequate coverage of congressional contests in the media, "members of Congress, and their opponents at election time, remain largely unknown to most of their constituents."[11] The evidence upon which this conclusion is based, however, consists entirely of data on incumbent saliency, narrowly defined—that is, measures of the respondents' ability to recall the candidates' names. These are the only systematic data on public knowledge of House incumbents and challengers that have been collected over the years, and they tell us little about how a citizen will react in the voting booth. Although there is a good deal of variation in the form of the ballot across the country, in every situation the voter is presented with the candidates' names. (In one state, Virginia, the political party affiliation of the candidates is not included.) A voter who is unable to recall the names of the candidates may nonetheless recognize them when presented with his ballot and have enough information to react positively or negatively.

---

[10] See Donald E. Stokes, "Parties and the Nationalization of Electoral Forces," in *American Party Systems: Stages of Political Development*, William Nisbet Chambers and Walter Dean Burnham, eds. (New York: Oxford University Press, 1967), pp. 182–202. Chapter 5 of this book contains a full exploration of this topic.
[11] Warren E. Miller and Teresa E. Levitin, *Leadership and Change: Presidential Elections From 1952 to 1976* (Cambridge, Mass.: Winthrop Publishers, Inc., 1976), p. 33.

Partly because Stokes and Miller were so convincing in their description of the abysmal ignorance of congressional electorates, and partly because the Center for Political Studies built an impressive time series on candidate saliency, most investigations of candidate influence on voting in congressional elections have examined only the ability of voters to recall the name of the candidates. No clearer illustration of this tendency can be found than the burgeoning literature on the advantage of incumbency in congressional elections.

Success in reelection campaigns is hardly a new experience for members of the House of Representatives. Historically House incumbents who seek reelection have done very well. What changed in the 1960s was the margin of victory for incumbents. David Mayhew was the first to point out the "vanishing marginals" phenomenon.[12] He observed that from the mid-1960s on fewer and fewer seats contested by incumbents were falling in what is usually considered the competitive zone, where the vote approaches fifty-fifty. More and more districts became insulated from national electoral change; they were sufficiently safe for one party or the other that a typical national swing was less likely than before to dislodge the incumbent.[13] Open seats, on the other hand, retained a more competitive structure. Mayhew, Cover, Erikson, Ferejohn, and Nelson, using both election returns and survey data, confirmed that this dramatic change in the competitiveness of congressional districts could be attributed to the increased value of incumbency.[14] But why were incumbents attracting more votes in the 1960s and 1970s than they had before?

Mayhew suggested three possible explanations: (1) incumbents have benefited from favorable redistricting decisions, which increased the number of majority partisans in their districts; (2) incumbents have gained political support by becoming more adept at advertising, credit-taking, and position-taking; and (3) incumbents have benefited fortuitously from the erosion of party loyalties—incumbency has replaced party as a voting cue.

---

[12] David R. Mayhew, "Congressional Elections: The Case of the Vanishing Marginals," *Polity*, vol. 6 (Spring 1974), pp. 295–317.

[13] Tufte characterizes this political fact as a declining vote/seat ratio. Edward R. Tufte, "The Relationship between Seats and Votes in Two-Party Systems," *American Political Science Review*, vol. 67 (June 1973), pp. 540–554.

[14] The most important sources are Mayhew, "Congressional Elections"; Cover, "Advantage"; Robert S. Erikson, "The Advantage of Incumbency in Congressional Elections," *Polity*, vol. 3 (1971), pp. 395–405; John A. Ferejohn, "On the Decline of Competition in Congressional Elections," *American Political Science Review*, vol. 71 (March 1977), pp. 166–176; and Candice J. Nelson, "The Effect of Incumbency on Voting in Congressional Elections, 1964–1974," paper presented at the Annual Meeting of the American Political Science Association, 1976.

Cover and Ferejohn have shown that redistricting fails to account for the increased advantage of incumbency, although doubtless there are specific cases where a "coalition of incumbents" has succeeded in making a competitive seat safe by redrawing district lines.[15] Investigation of the second and third explanations has been constrained by the lack of adequate data on public perceptions of congressional candidates. After demonstrating that a behavioral change (not just a decline in the number of strong partisans) in the electorate had disproportionately benefited incumbents, analysts turned to saliency as a measure of candidate-induced change. On its face, it seemed unlikely to account for change of any kind—neither incumbent saliency nor the gap between incumbent and challenger saliency had increased during the the past two decades. Working independently with CPS election study data but slightly different analysis strategies, Cover, Ferejohn, and Nelson arrived at the same conclusion: more often than in the past, partisan identifiers were defecting to vote for the incumbent even when they could not recall his name. Clearly candidate saliency did not explain the increased advantage of incumbency.[16]

So investigation of this significant political change reached an impasse. It seemed impossible to determine whether Mayhew's second or third explanation was a more accurate representation of reality— that is, whether the increase in incumbent reelection resources or the erosion of party loyalties at all levels of government was more important. Even if party ties have less meaning now than before, some explanation is required for the pro-incumbent bias of the defections. Either incumbents are better known and/or better liked now than before; or incumbency itself has become more revered by the public; or the advantage in visibility and reputation long held by incumbents, though not increased, now translates more profitably into votes because party ties are weaker.

We can safely dismiss the second of these possibilities: although incumbency is often treated as a phenomenon that has meaning at the level of mass opinion, there is actually no evidence that voters have

---

[15] Cover, "Advantage," pp. 36–46; Ferejohn, "Decline," pp. 167–168. However, some dispute on this issue remains. See, for example, Edward R. Tufte, "Communication," *American Political Science Review*, vol. 67 (March 1974), pp. 211–213, and David R. Mayhew, "Congressional Representation: Theory and Practice in Drawing the Districts" in *Reapportionment in the 1970s*, Nelson W. Polsby, ed. (Berkeley: University of California Press, 1971), chap. 7.

[16] At times it was even a distinct liability. Cover found that in 1958, 1964, and 1974, with the Democratic tide running strong, name recognition for incumbent Republicans led to a net loss of support for incumbents. "Apparently recognition need not carry a positive valence for congressional incumbents" (Cover, "Advantage," pp. 111–114).

views about incumbency as such or believe that it is a value to be maximized. The other two possibilities, however, are both plausible and compelling. Unfortunately, more appropriate recognition and reputation measures are needed to test their validity, and none are available for the crucial decade in which the advantage of incumbency increased. We have no way of knowing whether the public has altered its view of incumbents during the past ten or fifteen years; political scientists believed that there was little to be learned from public opinion on the subject of congressional candidates. With the benefit of hindsight, we can now argue forcefully for the inclusion in national election studies of congressional incumbent job ratings and candidate thermometers. An analysis of public attitudes toward the incumbent in one congressional district in Oregon suggests the efficacy of this approach: according to its findings, "visibility does not insure popularity" and "incumbency is an advantage because voters are generally satisfied with their elected representatives."[17]

If knowledge of public attitudes toward congressional candidates can help unravel the determinants of the increased advantage of incumbency, it can also help us understand why the advantage is not uniform. Most objective indicators of the incumbency effect are measures of central tendency such as the "sophomore surge," an adjusted mean swing in favor of incumbents seeking reelection for the first time.[18] A cursory glance at individual district swings reveals substantial variation about that mean. For example, the Democratic freshmen in the 95th Congress did very well in their first reelection effort in 1976: in a year when the mean national swing was about two percentage points in favor of the Republicans, the mean swing in favor of the freshmen Democrats was five percentage points. Yet some of these freshmen members picked up twenty-five percentage points or more over their 1974 totals, while others dropped more than ten percentage points. Moreover, this large range in swing is not an artifact of a few atypical cases. In other words, incumbency is a resource that members are more or less successful in translating into an electoral advantage. This variation cannot be explained by party or national electoral tides; it is obviously a function of forces distinctive to each district.

[17] Alan I. Abramowitz, "Name Familiarity, Reputation, and the Incumbency Effect in a Congressional Election," *Western Political Quarterly*, vol. 27 (December 1975), pp. 668–684.

[18] This was first proposed as a measure of the incumbency effect by Albert Cover and David Mayhew. See their "Congressional Dynamics and the Decline of Competitive Congressional Elections," in *Congress Reconsidered*, Lawrence C. Dodd and Bruce I. Oppenheimer, eds. (New York: Praeger, 1977), pp. 54–72.

The Nation, the District, and the Voter

Variation in swing is not confined to districts where incumbents are seeking reelection for the first time. On the contrary, as Donald Stokes pointed out some years ago, one of the ways in which U. S. congressional elections differ from British parliamentary elections is precisely in exhibiting a much greater diversity in swing from one election to the next. Moreover, Stokes estimated that in the 1950s roughly half of the total variation in the partisan division of the vote in congressional districts could be attributed to forces arising at the constituency level. That the absolute magnitude of the variance in party vote in the 1950s was at its lowest point in ninety years and, in Stokes's view, presaged a nationalization of electoral forces is less relevant to our discussion than the fact that the forces for electoral change in congressional elections remain primarily constituency-based.[19] While constituency-based forces have not received careful study heretofore, they certainly include the relative stature of the candidates and the effectiveness of their campaigns.

It is clear from the literature that the importance of public perceptions of congressional candidates (and of candidate-controlled factors generally) varies tremendously with the level of analysis (the nation, the district, the individual voter) and with the relative emphasis given to continuity and change. At the national level, the distribution of party identification in the electorate is critically important for understanding why the Democrats have consistently attracted a majority of the national two-party vote for Congress in recent times and why the range of variation in the national party division over the years is so small. But party identification is of little help in accounting for the interelection swing in the national two-party vote that, however moderate, does occur. Of course, *party* is not irrelevant to swing—even the impulse to "throw the rascals out" hinges on party accountability—but *party identification* may be.

As we have seen, public assessments of the performance of the President are another national source of electoral change in midterm elections. The relationship appears to be asymmetrical—negative evaluations convert more readily into votes against the President's party than positive evaluations into votes for it. The President's performance is judged largely by the prevailing economic conditions, with spe-

---

[19] Since Stokes does not present the historical series of the national and state components of the partisan vote for Congress, we are unable to determine if the *proportion* of variance arising from forces at the constituency level also declined over time. Stokes, "Parties," pp. 182–202.

cific economic issues moving on and off the agenda of public concern.[20] As for the coattail effect, the insulating force of incumbency and the growing divergence of presidential and congressional voting coalitions[21] noted in recent years might lead one to assume that it had diminished. Nonetheless, the national congressional vote is still somewhat sensitive to the relative strength of the presidential candidates; midterm election returns still reflect the receding of national tides running with the previous presidential contest. Whatever the precise influence of surge and decline and the presidential referendum, the most profitable avenues for seeking the causes of change in the national two-party vote for Congress bypass the individual constituencies. All the evidence suggests that national partisan swing is more than the sum of district swings generated entirely by local electoral forces.

At the level of the individual voter, party identification remains the best predictor of behavior, in spite of the increase in defection. Of course, it is important to remember that data have never been available to test rival explanations such as candidate preference. Moreover, we have been attempting to explain the voting behavior of a national congressional electorate. There is no guarantee that explanations of individual behavior based on a sample of the national electorate apply equally to all congressional districts. Levels of party defection might well vary across districts according to the strength of the opposing candidates, the presence of volatile local issues, and so on.

In the absence of longitudinal survey data, explaining change at the level of the individual voter usually means explaining party defection. We assume that the congressional votes of party identifiers and independent partisans consistent with their party identification need no further explanation; it is the votes that are inconsistent with party that concern us. One shortcoming of this analytic perspective is that it directs attention only to the candidates' failures in mobilizing their fellow partisans and ignores the extent to which they succeed. All of a candidate's efforts to develop and maintain support among his own partisans and the support he succeeds in attracting are left out, though they are central to the candidate and to the nature of representation. I will return to this point shortly.

Party defection in congressional voting appears to be related most strongly with incumbency. Cover has demonstrated that by the 1970s

---

[20] See, for example, Butler and Stokes's discussion of how the balance of payments replaced unemployment as the most politically relevant economic issue in Britain. David Butler and Donald Stokes, *Political Change in Britain*, 2nd college ed. (New York: St. Martin's Press, 1976), pp. 245–271.

[21] Walter Dean Burnham, "Insulation and Responsiveness in Congressional Elections," *Political Science Quarterly*, Fall 1975, pp. 411–435.

over three-quarters of all defections in contested districts where an incumbent was running favored the incumbent.[22] There is no direct evidence, however, on the extent to which it is public perceptions of incumbents that link incumbency to defection. In midterm elections, defection is prompted by negative evaluations of the President; in presidential elections it is related to the attractiveness of the presidential candidates, although the evidence on this point is mixed. Finally, while candidate saliency as measured by name recall does not account for the increased incumbency effect, it remains a determinant of defection—at least in open seats, where a voter is much more likely to defect from his own party's candidate if he recalls the name of the challenger. No other factors have been shown to be related to party defection by individual voters in the national congressional electorate. In fact, from the perspective of the individual voter in a national congressional electorate it all looks cut and dried: the vast majority of votes can be explained by party identification; those that cannot—the votes of defectors and Independents—are accounted for primarily by incumbency and, to a lesser extent, by assessments of the President (particularly his handling of the economy) or presidential candidates and the simple visibility of the congressional candidates. At this level of analysis, one finds little evidence that the candidates themselves can do much to influence the outcome.

The congressional district provides a very different vantage point for viewing the importance of the candidate's actions and the public's reactions. The competitiveness of a constituency—how close the vote is to being evenly split—is a function of the party distribution of the voters and of the increment of support generated by the candidates. The former has insured the existence of safe Republican and safe Democatic districts for many years. Prior to the 1960s the distribution of seats by party vote resembled a normal curve (although it has flattened out somewhat in the twentieth century), with most seats clustered in the competitive zone where the parties are approximately equal in strength. Mayhew showed that seats held by incumbents had become disproportionately safe Democratic or safe Republican, with far fewer of them marginal. More and more, incumbents had become insulated from national partisan swings.[23]

This new noncompetitive structure has not yet made its impact on turnover felt, largely because of the increase in retirements since 1972. In addition, however, the decline in the proportion of incumbents defeated in any given election has actually been modest; in 1974,

---

[22] Cover, "Advantage," p. 53.
[23] Mayhew, "Congressional Elections," pp. 297–305.

for example, the swing in the national vote (six percentage points Democratic) was accompanied by a net swing in seats no smaller than expected by twentieth-century standards. There are several reasons for this. It may be that if the popular vote swing is large enough, a number of safe seats move into the competitive range and insure a sizable seat swing. Perhaps more important is the fact, already noted, that national popular vote swings are not uniform. Many of the Republican incumbents defeated in 1974 suffered losses substantially greater than the national swing against their party; many who were in or close to the competitive range survived the 1974 election while colleagues thought to be safe were defeated.

The Determinants of Change

So what are the determinants of change in congressional district returns? To begin with, we know that there is a good deal of variation in swing across districts—indeed, that local forces account for more of the change in district returns than national forces.[24] Incumbency accounts for some of this variation, but we have also seen that incumbency translates very unevenly into electoral support. It is hard to avoid the conclusion that changes occur largely in response to local candidates and local issues. In some cases these merely modify national forces or give them a distinctive local cast. Schoenberger discovered, for instance, that the size of particular Republican congressional losses in the 1964 election was related to the extent of the incumbents' association with Goldwater's candidacy.[25] In 1972, the damage done by McGovern's candidacy to several Democratic congressmen in and around Wayne County, Michigan, was heightened by the presence of a straight party lever, by the salience of busing, which was associated with McGovern, and by the quality and effort of the Republican challengers. Finally, while Watergate and the Nixon pardon may have had less impact on the 1974 national vote for Congress than economic issues, they certainly influenced the fate of the Republican members of the Judiciary Committee who had been most outspoken in their defense of Richard Nixon.[26]

Other constituency forces are independent of national ones. They include the reputation of the candidates, the campaign effort, and vo-

---

[24] Stokes, "Nationalization." Also see evidence presented in Chapter 5.
[25] Robert A. Schoenberger, "Campaign Strategy and Party Loyalty: The Electoral Relevance of Candidate Decision-Making in the 1964 Congressional Elections," *American Political Science Review*, vol. 63 (June 1969), pp. 515–520.
[26] Gerald C. Wright, Jr., "Constituency Response to Congressional Behavior: The Impact of the House Judiciary Committee Impeachment Votes," *Western Political Quarterly*, vol. 30 (Sept. 1977), pp. 401–410.

latile local issues—all of which are to some extent within the control of the candidates themselves. The only evidence we have that sheds any light on these constituency forces comes from case studies of individual contests, which generally have more to say about elite actions than about public opinion.[27]

From the perspective of the candidate for Congress, the district is the most politically meaningful unit of analysis. In particular, the most recent interelection swing in the constituency vote is the focus of his attention, and infinitely more interesting to him than any political scientist's definition of the competitive zone. Incumbent congressmen assess their electoral vulnerability very differently from outside observers. Indeed, their mild paranoia is not without justification. Erikson, adopting a serial perspective on vulnerability, found that a substantial number of members enter Congress by defeating an incumbent and/or leave the House through defeat at the hands of a challenger. Moreover, the seats that change party hands are not concentrated in marginal districts; "a big victory margin in one year does not insure future electoral success."[28] Members of Congress are well aware that safe Republican seats can turn into safe Democratic seats and vice versa. They also know that a considerable proportion of the seats that change party hands each year move against the national tide. Incumbents and challengers concentrate on their own district swing, then, because it is most relevant to long-term electoral survival. An incumbent who falls from 65 to 55 percent in one election is likely to attract even more serious opposition in the subsequent election; a challenger who has had a near miss will more easily attract campaign resources the next time out. The candidates themselves have a good deal of influence on the size and direction of the district swing. Congressmen, at least, have been telling us so. Stokes and Miller reported that the vast majority of the congressmen they interviewed attributed their success in reelection to their own personal record and standing.[29] John Kingdon, noting a similar "congratulation" response among the victorious candidates in his Wisconsin study, pointed out that defeated candidates rationalized their situation by attributing the outcome to factors beyond their control.[30] This psychological adjustment of reality is a matter less of distortion of fact than of alternative emphasis—

[27] See, for example, Alan L. Clem, *The Making of Congressmen: Seven Campaigns of 1974* (North Seitmate, Mass.: Duxbury Press, 1976) and the sources cited therein.

[28] Robert S. Erikson, "Is There Such a Thing as a Safe Seat?" *Polity*, vol. 8 (Summer 1976), pp. 623–632.

[29] Stokes and Miller, "Party Government," p. 206.

[30] John Kingdon, *Candidates for Office: Beliefs and Strategies* (New York: Random, 1966), chap. 2.

incumbents and victors focus on the increments of support that are essential to long-term survival, challengers and losers on the stable elements in the constituency that usually favor the other party.

From this perspective it is clear why incumbents take so much care to develop and sustain their reputations among constituency groups. In his most recent research on congressmen in their constituencies, Richard Fenno describes how members develop distinctive "home styles" in order to win and hold voter support in their districts. Their subjective assessments of electoral safety are dominated by uncertainty—the threat of redistricting, of population shifts, of external events like recession or Watergate, but most important the unpredictability of the challenger. A congressman realizes that the political support base of this year's challenger may be very different from the support base of the last and that the composition of his own reelection constituency can change in response to a new challenger. "Home styles," especially the presentation of self, generate public trust, which helps members achieve some stability in the face of this uncertainty.[31] Its distinctly personal content sets home style in sharp contrast with the two other major sources of the public's view of congressmen, namely party and issues.

There can be no doubt that parts of the public are aware of one or both of the major party candidates for Congress in any given election and that their vote depends on the relative appeal of those candidates. Even if this "attentive electorate" is a distinct minority, it can influence the outcome of a congressional race. Unfortunately, we have little knowledge of the size of the attentive public in congressional elections or of the extent to which the visibility and appeal of the candidates influence the voting decisions of individuals or the final outcome. The reasons for underestimating or ignoring the importance of the individual candidates in congressional elections are diverse: inadequate measures; insufficient research on swing in district returns; the use of static and objective, rather than serial and subjective, measures of electoral vulnerability; the assumption that party-line voting is routine whatever the candidates do.

This research attempts to fill some of these gaps. It is directed specifically at public opinion in congressional elections and asks: How aware is the public of congressional candidates? What is it about the candidates that the public perceives? How does this influence their votes? How does public awareness of candidates vary across districts and over time? And to what extent are congressional elections district rather than national events?

---

[31] Richard F. Fenno, Jr., *Home Style: House Members in Their Districts* (Boston: Little, Brown, 1978).

3
Public Awareness of Congressional Candidates

Before assessing the impact of public perceptions of congressional candidates on individual vote choice and on electoral outcomes, I must first document what the public knows about the candidates. Donald Stokes and Warren Miller were impressed with how many voters in 1958 knew nothing at all about the candidates for the House of Representatives. Since the publication of their findings, no evidence has been presented to dispute the accuracy of this conclusion for the 1958 electorate or to support the view that the level of public information about congressional candidates has increased. The burden of proof is clearly on those who would argue that a significant part of the public is aware of the candidates.

The purpose of this chapter is to investigate the level and nature of public opinion in congressional elections, primarily by using surveys conducted for candidates by the Democratic Study Group in 1974 and 1976. The size of the "attentive public" in congressional elections and the content of their perceptions are the major targets of inquiry. I pay special attention to variations in candidate saliency—between incumbents and challengers, across districts, over time, and in response to the candidates' actions.

Candidate Saliency

In recent years the saliency of a congressional candidate has been taken to mean the proportion of the public that is able to recall his name. Stokes and Miller, however, conceived of candidate saliency in a broader context. The 1958 SRC Election Study questionnaire is the most extensive survey instrument dealing with public perceptions of Congress and congressional candidates ever administered to a national sample of U.S. citizens. In addition to including the item, "Do you happen to remember the name(s) of the candidate(s) for Congress that ran in this district this November?" (which has been repeated in most SRC/CPS election studies since that time), the 1958 questionnaire instructed the interviewers to provide respondents with the names of the candidates when asking them, "Now we're interested in knowing what sorts of persons people think these candidates are. Have you read or heard anything about (NAME OF CANDIDATE)?" The responses to the latter question provided the measure of saliency used by Stokes and Miller; it also served as a screen for a series of additional questions assaying the public's knowledge of the candidates. On its face this measure of saliency appears to be less demanding than the more conventional recall question alluded to above—it is easier to remember reading or hearing about a particular candidate than it is to remember his name. Yet just the reverse was true: more respondents correctly recalled the names of the candidates than indicated having read or heard anything about them.[1] In spite of their use of an "easier" test of saliency, Stokes and Miller might still have underestimated public awareness of the candidates by using this question format.[2]

Name Recall. Most investigators of candidate saliency since Stokes and Miller have relied upon measures of name recall, not candidate awareness. Gallup and Harris have normally asked, "Do you happen to know the name of the congressman from your district?" while the SRC/CPS format is "Do you happen to remember the names of the candidates for Congress that ran in this district this November?" Table 3-1 contains a number of time series on candidate saliency, all based on name recall. The differences in the findings for a given year stem primarily from differences in the bases used; while Ferejohn's figures are derived from voters in all contested seats, for example, Cover's come from voters and nonvoters in all seats contested by an incumbent. Obviously, Cover's figures are depressed by the inclusion of less attentive (nonvoting) members of the electorate.

Several things are apparent from these data. Incumbents are bet-

---

[1] Among voters in contested seats, 56 percent were able to recall the name of the incumbent and 35 percent the name of the challenger; the average name-recall score for candidates in open seats was 42 percent. The comparable figures for those responding affirmatively to the question "Have you read or heard anything about (NAME OF CANDIDATE)" are 49 percent for incumbents, 25 percent for challengers, and 34 percent for candidates in open seats. Almost 40 percent of those who correctly recalled the name of the candidate said they had *not* "read or heard anything" about that candidate. These figures are derived from the 1958 SRC election study, which was made available by the Inter-University Consortium for Political and Social Research.

[2] It may be that the prefatory sentence, "Now we're interested in knowing what sorts of persons people think these candidates are," led some respondents to think that they were being asked for intimate knowledge of the candidates.

Table 3-1
CONGRESSIONAL CANDIDATE SALIENCY MEASURES: NAME RECALL DATA FROM NATIONAL SURVEYS, 1942–1976
(in percentages)

Year	Gallup, Incumbent	Harris, Incumbent	Ferejohn (SRC/CPS) Incumbent	Ferejohn (SRC/CPS) Non-incumbent	Cover (SRC/CPS) Incumbent	Cover (SRC/CPS) Non-incumbent
1942	50					
1947	42					
1957	35					
1958			58	38	44	28
1964			63	40	52	32
1966	46		56	38	40	23
1968			64	47	50	34
1970	53		55	31	35	16
1972					36	19
1973		46				
1974					34	16
1976		50				

Note: The Gallup and Harris entries are percentages of all respondents in a national survey who recalled the name of their congressman. The Ferejohn entries are percentages of voters in all contested seats who recalled the names of the candidates. The Cover entries are percentages of all respondents in seats contested by an incumbent who recalled the names of the candidates.

Source: The Gallup data are reported in Cover, "Advantage," p. 56. The Harris data are taken from surveys commissioned by the Congress—in 1973 by the Senate Subcommittee on Intergovernmental Relations, in 1976 by the House Commission on Administrative Review. The Ferejohn data are taken from Ferejohn, "On the Decline," p. 170. The Cover data are computed from table 2.9 on page 58 of Cover, "Advantage."

ter known than nonincumbents; their advantage has remained roughly constant, around twenty percentage points, over the last two decades. There has been no increase in candidate name recall over this period; the decline that appears in Cover's data beginning in 1970 might be concentrated among nonvoters. In general, more than half of those voting in congressional elections are able to recall the name of the incumbent and a third or more recall the nonincumbent's name. These figures are slightly higher in presidential election years, when the level of political communication substantially increases.

How do these national figures distribute over congressional dis-

Table 3-2
CONGRESSIONAL CANDIDATE SALIENCY MEASURES: NAME RECALL DATA FROM PREELECTION DISTRICT SURVEYS, 1976

(in percentages; "advantage" figures in percentage points)

Type of Seat and Candidate	District Mean	Range
Seats contested by incumbents ($N = 24$)		
Incumbents	50	26 to 78
Challengers	25	5 to 63
Incumbent advantage	25	1 to 45
Open seats ($N = 4$)		
Candidates	22	11 to 38
Candidate advantage	4	0 to 6

Note: Incumbent advantage is defined as the percentage incumbent minus the percentage challenger. Candidate advantage is the absolute difference between the scores of the two candidates in an open seat.
Source: DSG surveys.

tricts? Is the name recall advantage of incumbents uniform, or is the distribution about the mean as notable as the mean itself? Table 3-2 summarizes the name recall readings obtained from surveys of likely voters conducted by the Democratic Study Group in twenty-eight marginal districts just prior to the 1976 election. (The name recall question used was roughly the same as that used by Gallup and SRC/CPS.) The mean incumbent, challenger, and incumbent-advantage scores computed for the twenty-four districts that were contested by an incumbent are close to Ferejohn's most recent figures, although the DSG figures, since they are taken from preelection surveys, no doubt underestimate the public visibility of candidates, especially challengers, on election day. But the district surveys allow us to see the considerable variation in these figures across congressional districts.

Most important, they show that, while incumbents generally have an impressive name recall advantage, in a few cases their advantage is almost nil. The name recall difference between opposing candidates in open seats, on the other hand, is exceedingly small.

The determinants of differences in levels of candidate name recall are difficult to unravel given the limited number of cases available for analysis. One primary determinant appears to be the nature of the media market in the given congressional district. At one extreme are districts embedded in very large metropolitan areas where public service coverage and paid political advertising of incumbents and challengers are severely restricted. This situation can apply to an entire state—New Jersey has no state-based television programming at all. At the other extreme are congressional districts whose boundaries are contiguous with a natural media market, assuring a reasonable amount of free coverage and cost-effective rates for paid advertising; Toledo, Ohio, is one such. In between these extremes are districts whose media markets present various opportunities and obstacles. A candidate's success in overcoming the obstacles depends in part on the availability of campaign funds and on his public relations skills. The three lowest name recall scores for incumbents were registered in districts that are located in greater metropolitan Los Angeles, New York City, and Chicago, and incumbents from New Jersey were well below the mean. Since all television and daily newspaper outlets in these districts blanket the entire metropolitan area, news coverage of congressional contests is limited and the cost of paid advertising prohibitive. The three highest name recall scores were obtained by congressmen whose districts entirely encompass middle-sized cities that have their own television stations and newspapers. This relationship can be verified by dividing the sample districts into three rough categories according to media access and then computing the mean name recall score for incumbents and challengers in each. The resulting figures meet every expectation: the mean name recall score for incumbents in districts with good media access is 61 percent; in districts with fair media access, 50 percent; in those with poor access, 41 percent. The comparable figures for challengers are 42 percent, 24 percent, and 17 percent.

Yet levels of candidate name recall are also influenced by the efforts of the candidates themselves. Another incumbent from the Chicago metropolitan area, who faced the same structural media problems as the congressman referred to above, was twenty-three percentage points ahead of his colleague on name recall. In the Washington, D.C. area two freshmen congressmen whose districts lie side by side had scores twenty percentage points apart. More dramatic evidence of the candidate's impact on his own saliency can be seen from the relative visibility of the challengers. The highest name recall figures for challengers were recorded by former incumbents, former challengers, and first-time candidates who invested heavily in cost-effective mass media. While the lowest challenger scores were found in the major metropolitan areas, many candidates in more attractive media markets also rated poorly on name recall.

There is some evidence that name recall increases with seniority, whatever the structure of the media market, although there are too few senior incumbents in my sample to test this proposition definitively. In several districts, freshman congressmen registered impressive gains in the year preceding their first reelection attempt after they sharply stepped up their use of mass mailings.

An analysis of the impact of candidate name recall on individual vote choice must await the next chapter. For now, it is sufficient to observe that it is probably unwise to rely exclusively on this single measure of candidate saliency. Several scholars have demonstrated that name recall cannot account for the increased ability of incumbents to attract partisan defectors; in the districts surveyed by the DSG, several candidates won in spite of the fact that fewer voters recalled their names than recalled their opponents' names.

An illustration from recent electoral history vividly demonstrates the limitations of this measure. In the summer of 1976 Representative Alan Howe, a first-term member of the House from Utah, was arrested in Salt Lake City for attempting to buy sexual favors from a police-woman disguised as a prostitute. The story attracted immediate national attention, and it remained in the news for some time as the drama of Howe's trial and his decision whether to stand for reelection unfolded. If ever a congressman was "salient," Alan Howe was in the summer of 1976. Yet when asked in August, "Can you tell me the name of your congressman," only 41 percent of a sample of his district's likely voters correctly identified Howe. This measure in no sense captured the level of public awareness of this congressman, nor did it elicit the direction and nature of the public's response to him. Table 3-3 presents figures summarizing Howe's visibility and popularity in November 1975 and August 1976. When presented with his name in August, virtually all respondents indicated that they recognized Howe; 73 percent reacted to him in a negative or positive way; and 65 percent provided a favorable or unfavorable rating of the job he was doing as a congressman. The public response to Howe's arrest was just what we would have guessed, but the traditional name recall measure could not accurately record it.

Name Recognition. At the very least, then, saliency measures must allow for the fact that some voters who are unable to recall the name of a candidate can still recognize the name when presented with it and can respond to it in a positive or negative fashion. What is the evidence on simple recognition of incumbents and challengers? The data summarized in Table 3-4 reveal that the electorate is more aware of congressional candidates than was previously thought. In thirty-one congressional districts surveyed by the DSG, virtually all voters recognized the name of the incumbent when they heard it, and most had a positive or negative response.

In 1974 the survey respondents were first read a list of names and

30

Table 3-3

VISIBILITY AND POPULARITY OF REPRESENTATIVE ALAN HOWE, NOVEMBER 1975 AND AUGUST 1976

(in percentages of respondents)

Measure	November 1975	August 1976
Name recall	19	41
Simple recognition	89	99
Thermometer		
Positive	31	12
Neutral	38	22
Negative	6	61
Job rating		
Favorable	43	29
Unfavorable	25	36

Note: Simple recognition is defined as 100 percent minus those who said they did not recognize Howe when asked to describe their feelings toward him on a five-point feeling thermometer. (They were explicitly instructed to say they did not recognize him if that were the case.) Positive, neutral, and negative scores were obtained directly from the five-point feeling thermometer on which one and two are negative, three is neutral, and four and five are positive. Favorable job rating includes "excellent" and "pretty good" responses to the question, "How would you rate the job Alan Howe is doing as congressman: excellent, pretty good, only fair, or poor?" "Only fair" and "poor" responses constitute an unfavorable job rating. The sequence of these items on the questionnaire was as follows: name recall, thermometer (with no prior mention of office or party), and job rating (with no prior mention of party).
Source: DSG surveys.

asked to indicate whether or not they recognized each; if the answer was yes, they were then asked whether they had a generally favorable or unfavorable opinion of that person. The six districts contested by incumbents were all represented by relatively senior Republicans who were subsequently defeated by their Democratic challengers in November. The mean incumbent advantage was fourteen percentage points for simple recognition and double that for recognition with evaluation. In these districts about 20 percent of the respondents in the case of incumbents and almost 40 percent for challengers claimed to recognize the name of the candidate but were unable to express a favorable or unfavorable view of him. This combination of responses is not entirely inconceivable—voters might recognize a candidate but be genuinely indifferent to him. It is likely that some respondents, however, claim to recognize names they don't know in order to appear informed or to please the interviewer. One means of checking this possibility is to see what recognition levels are recorded for candidates with very little or

Table 3-4
NAME RECOGNITION OF CONGRESSIONAL CANDIDATES, 1974 AND 1976
(in percentages; "advantage" figures in percentage points)

District Type and Year	Simple Recognition		Positive or Negative Response	
	Mean	Range	Mean	Range
Incumbent-contested seats				
1974 (*N* = 6 districts)				
Incumbents	98	94 to 100	78	66 to 87
Challengers	85	77 to 92	47	38 to 60
Incumbent advantage	14	6 to 22	30	16 to 44
1976 (*N* = 25 districts)				
Incumbents	92	74 to 98	61	35 to 77
Challengers	68	47 to 96	33	20 to 64
Incumbent advantage	25	−2 to 52	28	−1 to 52
Open seats				
1974 (*N* = 4 districts)				
Candidates	76	46 to 97	42	15 to 59
Candidate advantage	21	5 to 44	10	0 to 43
1976 (*N* = 4 districts)				
Candidates	76	62 to 97	41	26 to 63
Candidate advantage	7	0 to 22	10	1 to 30

Note: The 1976 measures of simple recognition and positive or negative response are defined in Table 3-3. The 1974 measures are described in the text. Incumbent advantage is defined as the percentage incumbent minus the percentage challenger. Candidate advantage is the absolute difference between the scores of the two candidates in an open seat.
Source: DSG surveys.

no public exposure. A good example can be found in a normally safe Democratic district in Michigan where in 1974 a senior incumbent faced a political unknown with virtually no organizational backing from his party or civic groups and with total campaign expenditures of under $1,000. A mid-September 1974 survey of likely voters in the district revealed that 84 percent did not recognize the candidate's name and only 4 percent had a favorable or unfavorable view of him. Even if one assumed that in this case the over-reporting of recognition were as high as ten percentage points, the error would not have to be regarded as intolerably high.

In 1976 respondents in twenty-five districts were asked to express their feelings toward the candidates on a five-point feeling thermometer that included an explicit neutral point. (They were instructed to say so if they did not recognize the name.) Twenty of the twenty-five districts were represented by first-term incumbents—hence the slightly lower simple-recognition score than was recorded for the relatively senior incumbents in the 1974 sample; the figures for the two years become comparable when only the five more senior incumbents in 1976 are included. However, the mean differences between 1974 and 1976 in the percentage of those who rate the candidates either positively or negatively stem partly from the different measures used in the two years; the 1976 measure is probably a better indicator of the attentive public. The incumbency advantage in visibility is equally decisive in 1976, although apparently it is possible for as few as a third of the voters to have positive or negative feelings toward an incumbent and a fifth toward a challenger in a marginal seat. Of course, the norm is a good deal higher and the variation across districts is substantial. The constraints on visibility imposed by the structure of the media are less telling for simple name recognition than for evaluative responses to candidates.

The visibility of candidates in open seats was about the same as that of challengers in districts with incumbents running, but the advantage of one candidate over another in open seats was much less than an incumbent's advantage over his challenger in 1976. In 1974 the relationship was just the opposite for simple recognition: the leading candidate in an open seat had a much larger advantage over his opponent than the incumbent had over his challenger in a contested one. Obviously, there are too few open seats in the sample to permit generalization.

The district surveys also reveal that the public awareness of serious and active nonincumbent candidates rises in the course of the campaign; simple-recognition increases of as high as fifty-five percentage points were observed in one district over a six-month period. Shifts are less dramatic for candidates who begin with a measure of visibility —former incumbents, well-known local officials, and so on. Since most of the surveys were conducted anywhere from two to six weeks prior to the election, the figures in Table 3-4 no doubt understate the visibility of the candidates—especially nonincumbents—on election day.[3]

Of course, these measures tell us nothing about the content of the public's perception of the candidates. At this point all I have demonstrated is that most voters recognize the candidates for the House and

---

[3] More evidence on changes over time is contained in the last section of Chapter 4.

many are able to express some feeling toward them. How they feel and what they see are different matters entirely. Three types of measures can be used to discern the direction and content of public perceptions of the candidates. Generalized affect is captured nicely by candidate feeling thermometers. Evaluations of the performance of the incumbent in office are gathered by standard job-rating measures. More specific elements of the image conveyed by the candidate to the public—personal characteristics, ideology, positions on issues—require a variety of measures.

Reputation. Donald Stokes and Warren Miller, investigating public perceptions of congressional candidates in 1958, found that, "In the main, recognition carries a positive valence; to be perceived at all is to be perceived favorably."[4] Evidence from the 1974 and 1976 district surveys supports an alternative view: while on balance most candidates are viewed positively, some evoke distinctly negative reactions from the electorate. A version of the CPS five-point feeling thermometer, adapted for use in the DSG telephone surveys, was used in 1976 to measure feelings toward the candidates; in 1974 the simpler measure ("Do you have a generally favorable or unfavorable opinion of [NAME OF CANDIDATE]") was employed. Table 3-5 shows the range of feelings about incumbents and challengers in thirty-one districts in 1974 and 1976. When interpreting these figures, it is important to bear in mind the differences between 1974 and 1976, both in terms of the sample (senior Republican incumbents who lost in 1974; primarily first-term Democratic incumbents who won in 1976) and in terms of the measures (no explicit neutral point in 1974). The 1974 figures reveal a sizable range in the reputation of incumbents, an incumbent advantage over challengers in the actual percentage of respondents rating the candidates positively, but a clear edge for the challengers in the relative number of positive and negative rankings. The incumbents had both more friends and more enemies than the challengers. In 1976 the incumbents held a clear advantage in visibility and reputation, lending support to the view that incumbents do well at the polls partly because the voters know and like them more than their challengers. These data suggest that public perceptions of challengers are important for understanding both the success of typical incumbents and the exceptions.

When the neutral, don't know, and no answer categories are excluded, the incumbents in 1974 and 1976 have equal ratings while the challengers are twenty percentage points apart; thus the difference in incumbent advantage in 1974 and 1976 stemmed entirely from the

---

[4] Stokes and Miller, "Party Government and the Saliency of Congress," p. 205.

Table 3-5

FEELINGS TOWARD CONGRESSIONAL CANDIDATES IN THIRTY-ONE DISTRICTS, 1974 AND 1976

(in percentages; "advantage" figures in percentage points)

| | Positive Feelings | | | | Negative Feelings, All Respondents | |
| | All respondents | | Respondents excluding neutral, don't know, and no answer | | | |
Year and Candidate	Mean	Range	Mean	Range	Mean	Range
1974 (N = 6 districts)						
Incumbents	54	39 to 63	70	53 to 79	24	16 to 35
Challengers	38	32 to 49	81	77 to 84	9	6 to 11
Incumbent advantage	15	6 to 31	11	−3 to 26	15	5 to 26
1976 (N = 25 districts)						
Incumbents	42	22 to 60	70	55 to 84	18	9 to 29
Challengers	17	8 to 39	51	32 to 76	16	6 to 32
Incumbent advantage	25	4 to 46	19	−7 to 46	3	−10 to 19

Note: The five-point feeling thermometer was used to ascertain positive and negative feelings in 1976; the question, "Do you have a generally favorable or unfavorable opinion of (NAME OF CANDIDATE)," with no explicit neutral point, was used in 1974. The positive and negative entries for all respondents are absolute percentages. The two middle columns, from which neutral, don't know, and don't recognize are excluded, show the balance of positive to negative feelings:

$$\frac{\% \text{ positive}}{\% \text{ positive} + \% \text{ negative}}.$$

Source: DSG surveys.

Table 3-6
FEELINGS TOWARD INCUMBENTS, BY PARTY IDENTIFICATION, 1976
(in percentages)

Respondent's Party Identification	Positive Feelings		Negative Feelings	
	Mean	Range	Mean	Range
Incumbent's party	61	54 to 74	9	4 to 17
Independent	43	32 to 52	16	4 to 28
Challenger's party (N = 10 districts)	30	21 to 41	31	15 to 47

Note: Feelings were recorded on the five-point feeling thermometer.
Source: DSG surveys.

challenger ratings. And the the latter, higher among the Democratic challengers in 1974 than among the primarily Republican challengers in 1976, is consistent with the strong national Democratic tide in 1974. While partisan feelings may be partly responsible for the high positive ratings of the Democratic challengers in 1974, it is important to remember that the measure of feelings toward the candidates was taken without reference to party or office. If party was a determining force, it was mediated by public knowledge of and feelings toward individual candidates.

The differences in public support among incumbents are not simply an artifact of the number of partisans in each district; the variation is large among incumbent partisans, Independents, and those who identify with the challenger's party (see Table 3-6). Incumbents do uniformly well among their own partisans, but their ability to evoke a positive response from Independents and those who identify with the challenger's party varies widely.

Finally, candidate ratings change over time. In 1974, senior incumbents saw their ratings deteriorate in the face of opposition during the campaign. Many first-term incumbents improved their reputations considerably in the year prior to the 1976 campaign. Challengers' ratings improved or deteriorated depending on the visibility and success of their campaigns.

Job Ratings. The public sometimes differentiates between a generalized feeling toward a political figure and an assessment of his performance in office. A good illustration of this is found in public attitudes toward Gerald Ford during his tenure as President: many more people had

Table 3-7
JOB RATINGS OF CONGRESSMEN, 1974 AND 1976
(in percentages)

	Favorable		Unfavorable	
Year	Mean	Range	Mean	Range
1974 (N = 6 districts)	55	41 to 62	38	30 to 51
1976 (N = 22 districts)	52	34 to 64	30	13 to 42

Note: For the survey question, see Table 3-3. The mean percentage of respondents who were unable to evaluate the job performance of their congressmen was 7 percent in 1974 and 18 percent in 1976.
Source: DSG surveys.

warm feelings toward him than approved of the job he was doing as a President. Job ratings for six congressmen in 1974 and twenty-two congressmen in 1976 are set forth in Table 3-7. Once again we see that most voters are able to judge the performance of congressmen in office and that their judgments are not uniform. The range in favorable ratings—about twenty percentage points in 1974 and thirty in 1976— is comparable to that recorded on the feeling thermometer. The six senior Republican incumbents in 1974 more than matched the mean favorable job ratings of the twenty-two incumbents in 1976 (eighteen of whom were freshmen Democrats), but the former group were also ahead by an average of eight percentage points in unfavorable ratings. If the four nonfreshmen in 1976 are excluded, the difference is even more pronounced. It seems that senior incumbents in marginal districts who face serious opposition are more likely to evoke unfavorable public reactions than first-term incumbents in similar situations. Familiarity can breed contempt. Only one of the twenty-eight incumbents received an overall unfavorable job rating: he had become especially visible in 1974 as a member of the House Judiciary Committee asserting the innocence of Richard Nixon, and his job ratings and electoral fortunes had suffered as a consequence.

Candidate Image

Mass public knowledge of congressional candidates declines precipitously once we move beyond simple recognition, generalized feelings, and incumbent job ratings. No clearer demonstation of this fact is to be found than in public responses to open-ended questions about the candidates. Stokes and Miller pointed out some years ago that "the popular image of the Congressman is almost barren of policy content. A long series of open-ended questions asked of those who said they had any information about the Representative produced mainly a collection of diffuse evaluative judgments: he is a good man; he is experienced; he knows the problems; he has done a good job; and the like."[5] Years later Abramowitz found much the same thing in his survey of public opinion in an Oregon congressional district: some respondents mentioned the incumbent's issue positions and constituency services, but half of the comments referred to his personal qualities.[6]

The format and purpose of the DSG candidate surveys prevented consistent use of open-ended questions, but the results obtained in two districts where they were used, both represented by freshmen congressmen, were in accord with earlier findings. Just under half of the respondents were unable to provide a reason for liking or disliking the incumbent. In both districts favorable comments about the incumbent outnumbered unfavorable ones by better than three to one. The respondents who did comment emphasized primarily either personal qualities or relationships with constituents. The number of references to issues was very small by comparison, and they were disproportionately negative, which suggests that when issues are sufficiently salient to affect the public's image of the incumbent, they probably do the incumbent more harm than good.

Another way of getting at the candidates' public images is to ask respondents to judge the accuracy of a series of personal characterizations of the candidates. This might take the form of either, "Do you think Congressman X is _____?" or "Which candidate for Congress, X the Republican or Y the Democrat, do you think is more _____?" This question format allows the researcher to discern whether the public perceives the candidates in terms of the same attributes that the candidates themselves have attempted to present to the public. The difficulty is the confounding presence of nonattitudes—do the responses reflect real perceptions or are they merely guesses? One way of validating the pattern of responses is to look for a high degree of discrimination, either in the respondents' assessments of different characteristics for the same candidate or in their assessments of the same characteristic for different candidates. The degree to which a candidate evokes atypical responses compared to other candidates or responses that are highly differentiated over a number of image components is another measure of candidate saliency.

[5] Ibid., p. 207.
[6] Abramowitz, "Name Familiarity," p. 678.

Of course the initial hurdle—responding affirmatively or negatively to the personal-characterization question or judging which candidate most clearly has the stated quality—must be crossed before a pattern of responses can be analyzed. The percentage of respondents who "don't know" (DK) ranges from 15 to 75 percent, roughly in this order: long-term incumbents, 15 to 25 percent DK; new incumbents, 20 to 45 percent DK; challengers with prior exposure, 40 to 60 percent DK; and new challengers, 60 to 75 percent DK. Specific placement within these ranges is a function of the individual candidate and of the type of attribute. For example, in 1976 the average percentage of respondents who didn't know whether a series of personal qualities accurately fit one freshman congresswoman was 20 percent; the average "don't know" response for another freshman congresswoman was 45 percent. Part of this difference can be attributed to the extent of media access in each district (the latter represented a district in which the use of television was virtually impossible), part to the initiative and skill of the individuals. The number of respondents unable to comment is sensitive also to the nature of the characterization. The percentage responding "yes" or "no" on qualities like "honest" and "hard working" and "listens to the people" is uniformly higher than the percentage for qualities like "doesn't care about the environment" or "is too friendly with the banking industry." The same candidate might evoke only 20 percent DK responses to questions about his character but 50 percent DK to questions about his policy stands. It seems that the public has sufficient information (or is willing to assume the best) about candidates' overall integrity and responsiveness, but that it is largely unaware of these candidates' performance in specific policy areas.

Several examples show that the public is able to judge congressional candidates on several attributes. In 1974 a senior Republican incumbent who had long enjoyed a reputation for excellent constituency service faced a challenger whose campaign focused primarily on "good government" issues—disclosure of campaign contributions and personal income, sunshine in congressional committees, and the like. A survey taken six weeks before the election revealed that while only 6 percent of the respondents took the incumbent to task for not working hard enough and 11 percent found him lacking in honesty, 47 percent believed him to be "too close to special interests." This is precisely the view of the incumbent that had been articulated for many years by his Democratic challengers; it seems that some of the voters were listening.

Another illustration is drawn from a Midwestern urban district represented for many years by a Democrat. After repeatedly winning

39

reelection by wide margins, this incumbent almost lost in 1974 despite the strong national tides favoring the Democratic party. In 1976 he faced the same Republican challenger, whose campaign once again emphasized the importance of change and the need for congressional reform. The Democratic incumbent countered with a strong attack on the personal stability and qualifications of the challenger. A survey of likely voters found that while most believed the Democrat to be "more qualified to hold public office" (55 percent to 16 percent), a large plurality of voters (44 percent to 27 percent) thought the Republican challenger "would try hardest to reform Congress." Once again, public opinion reflected the images articulated by the candidates.

A third example involves a first-term Democrat who had unseated a Republican incumbent after the latter had spent two terms in the House. The Democrat, a political neophyte prior to her narrow victory in 1974, faced the same opponent in her first reelection bid. One month before the election the Republican was perceived to be "more experienced" (55 percent to 18 percent) while the Democrat was judged "more honest" (40 percent to 11 percent) and "more likely to try to help people around here" (58 percent to 20 percent). In this case a large number of voters knew that the Republican had considerable experience in office, at least more than the Democrat. Yet they were able to differentiate experience from responsiveness or attractiveness on other qualities.

In all three cases, the qualities (or alleged qualities) of the candidates that were part of the political dialogue in the constituency became elements of the candidate images perceived by the public. No detailed knowledge of the candidates was required of voters, only the barest recognition and general sense of the candidates conveyed in the media. Obviously the entire electorate did not respond to these images, but at least a third to half were sufficiently aware to hold a multifaceted view of the candidates. It appears that the public was able to discriminate between the contenders and that its views make sense in the light of what we know about the candidates.

In all of these districts the campaigns were lively and hard-fought. The pattern of public responses to candidate images in other districts is much more uniform. In the absence of any controversial actions that focus public attention on the incumbent and lacking a challenger who attacks the personal failings of his opponent or dramatically embodies an alternative, candidate images consist solely of positive or (much less frequently) negative recognition. The range in negative responses to personal characterizations of a single candidate or in the advantage of a candidate over his opponent in these districts is barely ten percentage points, compared with the forty to fifty percentage-point range for the salient candidates discussed above. Incumbents have a distinct advantage in districts where the public's view is undifferentiated; constituents generally believe their representative is honest and responsive and concerned about their problems, and this is usually enough to stem criticism on substantive grounds.[7]

Assessments of the same personal quality over a number of districts seem to vary less. For example, the range in negative assessments of whether candidates were "hard working" was six percentage points and whether they were "honest," ten percentage points. In 1974, larger differences were obtained for "rubberstamp for President Nixon" (fourteen percentage points) and "too conservative" (twenty-two percentage points), neither of which can be explained simply by the number of partisans in each district. Apparently candidates can act to heighten the public's association between themselves and national political figures or broad ideological positions.

Ideology

This raises a related question: To what extent is the electorate aware of the general ideological stance of congressional candidates and how important is this for individual vote choice and for electoral outcomes? In practical politics, the electoral relevance of a candidate's ideology is taken as self-evident. The ideological complexion of a district is thought to impose constraints on a candidate that, if he violates them, mean his defeat. For example, it is often said that, Democrats from the Eastern Shore of Maryland are socially and economically conservative; a liberal candidate hasn't a chance of victory there. Democrats from North Carolina, Tennessee, Indiana, and New Jersey first elected to the House in 1974 by defeating Republican incumbents speak openly of the importance of living within the predominant ideological orientation of their districts, and their voting in Congress reflects that decision.

Yet there are many reasons why we would expect not to find much evidence in public opinion of an ideological influence on congressional voting. The first is the extensive body of research demonstrating the nonideological character of political thinking in the mass public. We know that most citizens' orientation to parties and political figures has

---

[7] The same cannot be said for public ratings of the Congress itself. We have only begun to understand why ratings of congressmen and the Congress diverge so dramatically. See, for example, Richard F. Fenno, Jr., "If, As Ralph Nader Says, Congress is a Broken Branch, How Come We Love Our Congressmen So Much?" in *Congress in Change*, Norman Ornstein, ed. (New York: Praeger, 1975), pp. 277–287, and Fenno, *Home Style*.

little ideological content, changes in the 1960s and 1970s notwithstanding. Second, ideology is not unidimensional. At the very least, ideology encompasses cultural, economic, and foreign policy dimensions, and candidates are often as ideologically inconsistent in these areas as the public. Third, ideology would not enter the electorate's calculus if both candidates were ideologically acceptable. In this sense, ideology serves as a screen in the recruitment of candidates; after the recruitment stage, it is effectively removed from the political debate. Fourth, candidates' ideological stances might be perceived only by the most politically attentive stratum. What reaches the mass public might be a simple positive or negative message devoid of ideological content. Under these circumstances, ideology is very important electorally to candidates, but scarcely a trace of its influence can be detected in public opinion.

No attempt was made in the DSG candidate surveys to determine the levels of conceptualization of the electorate. Rather, respondents were asked either to describe the political views of the candidates as liberal, moderate, or conservative or to judge whether a candidate was too liberal or too conservative. No doubt these labels have very different meanings for different people, but they do provide some measure of whether congressional candidates are ideologically visible to the public. Table 3-8 shows the extent to which congressional electorates were able to describe candidates as liberal, moderate, or conservative. While on the average three-quarters of the public was able to label incumbents in this fashion, no more than half could describe the ideological stance of challengers, except when the challenger was a former incumbent. The average ideological-visibility advantage of incumbents over challengers was twenty-eight percentage points; in open seats the mean difference between candidates was twelve percentage points.

Of course, these perceptions might be nothing more than guesses —rationalizations whereby voters project their own ideological views onto the candidates—or routine expressions of partisan loyalties. In fact, there is some evidence of obvious misperception—5 percent of the respondents in one district described a very conservative incumbent as liberal and 6 percent in another district labelled a liberal challenger as conservative. Overall, however, the balance of ideological perceptions for each candidate makes sense.[8] This fact is due partly but not entirely to the mediation of party labels. If we examine only the bal-

---

[8] The test here and below is the author's knowledge of the positions on issues taken by the candidates in their campaigns and by incumbents in the Congress.

Table 3-8
PUBLIC AWARENESS OF THE IDEOLOGICAL STANCE OF CONGRESSIONAL CANDIDATES, 1974 AND 1976
(in percentages; "advantage" figures in percentage points)

Type of Seat and Candidate	Respondents Describing Candidate as Liberal, Moderate, or Conservative	
	Mean	Range
Seats contested by incumbents (N = 12)		
Incumbents	73	63 to 89
Challengers		
Former incumbents (N = 2)	69	66 to 73
Other (N = 10)	43	28 to 50
Incumbent advantage	28	−3 to 43
Open seats (N = 12)		
Candidates	42	15 to 43

Note: Incumbent advantage is defined as the percentage describing the incumbent as liberal, moderate, or conservative minus the percentage describing his challenger as liberal, moderate, or conservative.
Source: DSG surveys.

ance of liberal to conservative ratings, a clear party difference emerges (see Table 3-9). For Democratic candidates the average difference is nine percentage points more liberal than conservative ratings, while for Republican candidates it is sixteen percentage points more conservative; the mean liberal/conservative difference between incumbents and challengers is twenty-five percentage points. (Remember, these percentages are computed on a base of all respondents, including those who describe the candidate as moderate or who "don't know.") Once again, there is considerable variation about the mean for each party. The most conservative Democratic candidate received the most conservative rating among Democrats; the most liberal Republican candidate received the most liberal rating among Republicans. The absolute liberal/conservative difference between incumbents and challengers ranged from zero to thirty-nine percentage points.

The figures reported in Table 3-9 are derived entirely from 1976 surveys in which a three-point liberal, moderate, and conservative scale was used. In 1974 the Republican incumbent who most vocally and visibly advertised his conservative credentials was described by 70

Table 3-9
LIBERAL/CONSERVATIVE IMAGES OF CONGRESSIONAL CANDIDATES, 1976
(in percentage points)

Candidate's Party	Percentage ''Liberal'' Minus Percentage ''Conservative''	
	Mean	Range
Democrat	9	—10 to 25
Republican	—16	5 to —34
Absolute difference (N = 8 districts)	25	0 to 39

Source: DSG surveys.

percent of the voters in his district as "somewhat conservative" or "very conservative." The public seems to respond predictably when the signals from the candidates are sufficiently clear.

This difference among candidates is maintained when the form of the question is altered. The percentage of respondents who demonstrated ideological distance from candidates by responding affirmatively to the question "Do you think (NAME OF CANDIDATE) is 'too liberal'?" (or "too conservative") ranged from 5 percent to 32 percent.

There is certainly enough evidence here to warrant an investigation of the influence of ideology on congressional voting. I reserve that task for the next chapter.

Issues

Assessing the impact of specific issues on voting in congressional elections is more problematic. The requirements for policy voting discussed by Warren Miller and his colleagues and by Richard Brody and Benjamin Page (the issue must be salient to the voters, the candidates must be perceived to take different issue positions, the voters must have real issue preferences, and the voters must choose the most proximate candidate) are much more rarely met at the congressional than at the presidential level.[9] A major stumbling block to policy voting in congressional elections is the requirement that the candidates be perceived to take different positions on a given issue. In order for

[9] Campbell, Converse, Miller, and Stokes, *American Voter*, chap. 8; Richard A. Brody and Benjamin I. Page, "The Assessment of Policy Voting," *American Political Science Review*, vol. 66 (June 1972), pp. 450–458.

candidates to be so perceived, they must visibly disagree on issues that are highly salient to the voters. But many of the incentives that influence candidates invite agreement, not disagreement. John Kingdon has demonstrated that, through the mechanisms of recruitment and "explaining"—justifying their votes before constituent groups—congressmen most often adopt the dominant constituency opinion, in so far as it can be determined.[10] This is especially true for salient local issues such as busing, farm policy, and gun control. Challengers in particular have little to gain by taking opposing positions and articulating their differences with the incumbent.[11] In the absence of the necessary political communication, the public remains unaware of the positions of the candidates. Their becoming aware usually means trouble: as Kingdon puts it, "If constituents were better informed, it would probably be a mark of arousal over something that the congressman did which was out of keeping with their strongly held beliefs."[12]

The public's ignorance of the positions congressional candidates take on issues can be largely explained by the way in which the candidates themselves exploit the issues. In addition to respecting whatever policy constraints are imposed by mass opinion in their constituencies, candidates often avoid taking ideological positions in dealing with issues. They are inclined to emphasize their interest in reducing inflation *and* restoring the economy to full-employment, cutting wasteful government spending *and* maintaining a strong national defense, preventing abuses by public bureaucracies *and* by private corporations. More attention is paid to consensual goals than divisive means. All this does little to educate the public on the respective positions of the candidates. Candidates also use issues more to demonstrate their competence than to spell out clear positions on substance. The manner in which they deal with issues is more likely to be conveyed to the public than the content of their commitments. Of course, elites pay attention to the positions of candidates, and issues are very important for attracting and maintaining core supporters, financial resources, and volunteers. But none of this necessarily informs the mass public about where a candidate stands on a specific issue.

---

[10] John W. Kingdon, *Congressmen's Voting Decisions* (New York: Harper and Row, 1973), chap. 2.

[11] Actually, the distribution of public opinion determines the rationality of taking opposing positions. While in homogeneous districts the candidates' positions seem likely to converge, there is some theoretical and empirical evidence suggesting that it is rational for candidates to stake out opposing positions in heterogeneous districts. See Morris P. Fiorina, *Representatives, Roll Calls, and Constituencies* (Lexington, Mass.: D. C. Heath, 1974), chap. 5.

[12] Kingdon, *Congressmen's Voting Decisions*, p. 40.

Most of the candidates for whom DSG surveys were commissioned expected policy voting to be relatively unimportant in their races. For this reason no systematic measures of issue proximity were gathered in the DSG surveys. What little evidence is available confirms the view that most voters are unaware of the issue positions of the candidates. I have already discussed the paucity of references to issues in the responses to open-ended questions about the candidates. Even on controversial issues such as abortion and gun control, 70 to 80 percent of the voters surveyed in 1976 did not know the positions of the candidates for Congress. Seven out of every ten voters in a congressional district represented by a very visible Republican member of the House Judiciary Committee did not know what position he had taken on the Nixon pardon, although most were aware of his views on impeachment. At the height of the busing controversy in the Detroit suburbs, two-fifths of the voters in one congressional district had no idea what position their congressman had taken on the issue and three-fourths were unaware of the challenger's position. In this case, the voters' cues were confusing, because busing was both a national *and* a local issue, and because both congressional candidates opposed busing while the Democratic presidential candidate and the senior Democratic senator were on record in favor. The issue worked to the detriment of the Democratic congressional candidates in the Detroit area without the requirements for policy voting being met at the constituency level.

This last example demonstrates that issues can operate in very complex ways to influence the vote for Congress. Ultimately however, we should be able to trace the effect of an issue as it is mediated by feelings toward the congressional candidates or, at the national level, by assessments of the presidential candidates or incumbent administration. A more direct assessment of the role of issues is not possible given the limitations of the data.

Although the public's knowledge of congressional candidates is limited, the evidence presented in this chapter cautions against exaggerating the ignorance of the congressional electorate. The public responds to the political communication about the candidates that reaches its attention. When the major media in a congressional district convey little information about the candidates and when the candidates themselves fail to openly articulate clear differences, public awareness is low. Yet even where information is scarce, incumbents are able to increase their visibility and improve their reputations by plying the tools of their trade: constituency service, newsletters, direct mail, and so on. In many other districts, the constraints on candidate saliency imposed by the structure of the media are not so severe that money and ingenuity cannot overcome them. In these situations challengers as well as incumbents can reach enough of the electorate to move sizable numbers of voters into their column.

Large numbers of voters do have impressions of the candidates, however partial and fragile is the information at hand. Feelings can sour—quickly, in the wake of a devastating and widely publicized event, or gradually, as relations with elite groups become strained and effective opposition is mobilized. The relative visibility and reputation of the candidates condition the electoral influence of such important factors as party identification and the performance of the administration.

4

Candidate Image and Electoral Choice

The electoral relevance of public perceptions of congressional candidates can be investigated at two levels: the voter and the district. My plan in this chapter is to examine the relationship between public opinion and electoral choice as reflected in the attitudes and behavior of individual voters in ten congressional districts. In the next chapter the unit of analysis will shift to the congressional district, permitting an assessment of the determinants of outcomes of congressional elections—both the actual vote and the interelection swing.

The data presented in Chapter 2 made clear that most votes cast for the House of Representatives are consistent with party identification. Although in recent years partisan defection and Independent voting have been increasing, almost three-fourths of all votes for Congress are party-line votes. This empirical fact raises a critical strategic question for this chapter: What individual votes need to be explained? The need to account for votes cast by Independents and by those who stray from their traditional party loyalties is obvious. But what of the partisans who vote for congressional candidates of their own party? Is the successful mobilization of one's fellow partisans routine and automatic or does it require efforts by candidates that reach the public's consciousness? At the very least, it is important to determine the extent to which party-line votes are mediated by assessments of the candidate. Moreover, the variation in defection rates across congressional districts should provide some clues about the prerequisites for party-line voting in congressional elections.

The analytic strategy adopted here calls for treating partisan defection and Independent voting as the primary dependent variables, various measures of candidate visibility and reputation as the independent variables. In addition, a simple vote-choice model is used to assess the relative importance of party identification and candidate preference and the extent to which party-line votes are cast by voters who rate their party's candidate higher than his opponent without regard to party. Once again, I pay special attention to variations in these relationships: between incumbents and challengers, across districts, and over time.

A Brief Methodological Detour

All of the congressional district surveys used in this analysis were conducted prior to the elections; our data include no postelection reports of actual behavior, only turnout intentions and vote intentions expressed before the fact. The timing of these surveys has both advantages and disadvantages. On the positive side, measures of candidate visibility are not contaminated by the voting act itself—that is, respondents do not remember a candidate's name because they voted for him. Cover, trying to gauge the influence of candidate name recall on partisan defection, was confronted with the possible reciprocal influence of vote choice on name recall; since both measures were taken at the same time, he had to rely on a complex model to determine which was cause and which effect.[1] This problem is avoided here.

But there are several clear costs as well. The last survey in each district was conducted from two to six weeks before the election. Any real changes that took place in response to political stimuli after the survey was made obviously are not reflected in the data. Moreover, the ultimate behavior of those who were undecided about the contest for the House at the time of the last survey is unknown. Did they actually vote on election day? If they were partisans, did they simply vote their party? Are our estimates of partisan defection and Independent voting distorted since they fail to account for candidate switching late in the campaign and for the disposition of the undecided voters?

One way of approaching this problem is to compare the congressional vote-intention data from the final survey in a given district with the election results. What we find is that the final survey is an excellent predictor of the incumbent's vote, but that the challenger's actual vote increased over his percentage in the survey by an amount roughly equivalent to the number of undecided voters. The following figures (for twenty districts in 1976) demonstrate this point:

Mean percentage of undecided voters in final DSG survey	21
Mean difference between election returns and standing in final DSG survey (in percentage points)	
Incumbents	+ 4
Challengers	+17

---

[1] Cover, "Advantage," pp. 104–106.

If we are willing to assume that no changes occurred among those who expressed a candidate preference in the final survey and that all undecided voters ultimately voted, then only one conclusion can follow: challengers captured the vast preponderance of votes cast by those who were still undecided late in the campaign.[2] Allocating undecided voters along party lines or throwing them out altogether would lead one to underestimate the actual vote challengers obtained on election day.

What accounts for this challenger surge and how does it affect an analysis based on the final survey? A clue can be found in those cases that do not fit this pattern—open seats and seats in which the incumbent is challenged by a former incumbent. In both of these situations, neither candidate gains disproportionately between the final survey and the election. (Alternatively, one might say that the candidates divide the undecided vote evenly, if one is comfortable with the assumptions spelled out above.) What distinguishes these contests from those in which an incumbent faces a new challenger is the relative visibility of the candidates. Ordinarily former incumbents are as visible as new incumbents, and one candidate in an open seat is as visible as his opponent. In the typical incumbent-challenger contest, by contrast, the incumbent maintains a considerable advantage in visibility late in the campaign. Compared with the challenger, the incumbent is a known quantity; since voters have been exposed to political communication from and about the incumbent at least throughout the two-year term preceding the election, it is unlikely that their views toward him will alter appreciably at the tail end of the campaign. The challenger, on the other hand, suffers from lower recognition at the time of preelection surveys, which might cause one to underestimate his base party support and the benefit he might gain from national electoral tides. During the last stages of the campaign, the challenger can become more widely known to the electorate, prompting a return of some of his own partisans who had intended to defect and a favorable movement of undecided voters.[3] But even if the challenger's visibility does not increase markedly at the end of the campaign, he is still likely to enjoy the votes of those who were not sufficiently motivated to support the incumbent earlier in the campaign.

While this finding is interesting in and of itself, it complicates the analysis of candidate image and electoral choice. In order to explore these problems, it is useful to distinguish between a potential error

---

[2] It will soon become clear that the subsequent analysis does not depend upon these assumptions.

[3] This possibility is corroborated by the changes in challenger visibility and support measured between surveys earlier in the campaign. See Chapter 3 and the last section of this chapter on this point.

in the *absolute levels* of partisan defection and Independent voting and a potential distortion of the *relationship* between public opinion and vote choice arising from the use of preelection surveys. To examine the sources of error in the first of these, the level of defection and the vote choice of Independents, it is useful to begin by breaking down the electorate into all possible party-identification and vote-choice groups. At the time of the final preelection survey, every voter would fall into one of the following nine categories:

- identifies with the incumbent's party and intends to vote for the incumbent,
- Independent, intends to vote for the incumbent,
- identifies with the challenger's party and intends to vote for the incumbent,
- identifies with the incumbent's party and intends to vote for the challenger,
- Independent, intends to vote for the challenger,
- identifies with the challenger's party and intends to vote for the challenger,
- identifies with the incumbent's party and is undecided about whom to vote for,
- Independent, is undecided about whom to vote for,
- identifies with the challenger's party and is undecided about whom to vote for.

Throughout this chapter, I will be concerned primarily with partisan defection and with the votes of Independents who preferred a candidate. The problem is to know how voters still undecided at the time of the final survey actually voted.

A few preliminary observations can be made. First, more Independents than partisans are undecided at the time of the last survey; among partisans, more voters of the challenger's party than of the incumbent's are undecided. Second, the challenger's success in mobilizing his own party identifiers who were previously undecided will not alter the level of defection to the incumbent among the challenger's partisans. Third, some undecided voters who identify with the incumbent's party may vote for the challenger, but they will be few since the undecided group among the incumbent's party identifiers is always small. And fourth, more undecided Independents will vote for the challenger than for the incumbent, though many will abstain.

In addition, it is possible that some voters who expressed a vote choice at the time of the final survey will change their minds before the election, after acquiring some new information about one or both candidates. It is least likely that voters identifying with the incumbent's party who initially chose the incumbent will switch to the challenger; possible that some Independents who initially chose the incumbent will switch to the challenger; and most likely that some voters identifying with the challenger's party who initially chose the incumbent will switch to the challenger.

When both the disposition of undecided voters and changes in vote choice before election day are taken into account, we may conclude that the final preelection surveys provide good if slightly low estimates of defection among voters who identify with the incumbent's party, that they overstate defection among those who identify with the challenger's party to the extent that the challenger becomes more visible after the final survey, and that they provide a somewhat high estimate of incumbent support among Independents. It appears that some error arises from using preelection data as a surrogate for estimates of actual voting behavior, but that the amount is not too damaging.

On the other hand, the relationship between public opinion and vote choice is not vulnerable to most of the error introduced by preelection measurements, since both the movement of undecideds against their party and of partisans from their own to the other party would be accompanied by changes in public attitudes toward the candidates. In summary, even though the percentage of the vote for the challenger increases markedly between the final survey and election day, the use of these preelection data should not seriously distort the analysis of *the relationship between candidate saliency and vote choice.*

Levels of Partisan Defection and Independent Voting

Almost one-third of all votes cast for Congress in the ten congressional districts under investigation in this chapter[4] were other than party-line votes, that is, either defections by partisans or votes by Independents. This suggests that the constraints on congressional voting imposed by partisan loyalties are far less severe than has been assumed in the past. Tables 4-1 and 4-2 set forth measures of partisan defection and voting by Independents. Three of the four mean scores (percentage of incumbent partisans that defect, percentage of all defections favoring the incumbent, and percentage of all votes cast that are defections) are quite close to comparable figures computed from national samples by Cover and by Arseneau and Wolfinger.[5] The defection rate for chal-

---

[4] The ten districts were selected in an entirely arbitrary fashion. They were the only districts contested by an incumbent for which raw data were available to me. These districts were represented by seven first-term Democrats, a second-term Republican, a senior Republican, and a senior Democrat.

[5] Cover, "Advantage," pp. 49–54; Arseneau and Wolfinger, "Voting Behavior in Congressional Elections," p. 10.

Table 4-1

THREE MEASURES OF PARTISAN DEFECTION IN TEN CONGRESSIONAL RACES, 1976

(in percentages; "advantage" figures in percentage points)

Measure of Defection	Mean	Range
Percentage of partisans who defect		
Incumbent partisans	11	4 to 20
Challenger partisans	31	14 to 41
Incumbent advantage	21	3 to 37
Percentage of all defections favoring		
incumbents	71	36 to 88
Defections as a percentage of all		
votes cast	17	11 to 23

Note: Incumbent advantage is defined as the percentage challenger-partisan defection minus percentage incumbent-partisan defection.
Source: DSG surveys.

lenger partisans, 31 percent, is a good deal smaller than Cover's most recent figures (56 percent in 1972 and 49 percent in 1974). The difference probably stems from the nature of the sample used here—marginal districts are more likely to feature active and serious challengers than safe districts, and serious challengers are more likely to hold their own partisans in contests with incumbents. Cover's figures are based on a sample of all districts contested by incumbents, not just marginal ones. The difference might also reflect a real change in 1976 toward greater party voting among challenger partisans.

Defection rates for both incumbent and challenger partisans vary a good deal across the ten districts, although in no case does the rate among incumbent partisans exceed that among challenger partisans. The incumbent advantage was below the mean in only three districts: one contested by a former incumbent (three percentage points), one contested by a previous challenger who had waged a nearly successful campaign two years earlier (ten percentage points), and a final district in which a new but highly visible challenger defeated the senior incumbent (eleven percentage points). Occasionally the party profile of a district is such that the challenger has an advantage in the percentage of all defections in spite of the incumbent's advantage in defection rates. For example, a senior Democratic incumbent lost 20 percent of his partisans compared to his opponent's loss of 30 percent of the Republicans, yet the larger number of Democrats in the district meant

Table 4-2

VOTING BY INDEPENDENTS IN TEN CONGRESSIONAL
RACES, 1976

Measure	Mean	Range
Votes cast by Independents as a percentage of all votes cast	15	8 to 24
Percentage of all votes cast by Independents favoring incumbents	68	50 to 90

Source: DSG surveys.

that the challenger actually enjoyed a slight advantage among partisan defectors.

The mean percentage of all votes that were cast by Independents—15 percent—is about five percentage points higher than estimates derived from national surveys. The source of this difference could be any combination of a number of factors: some nonvoting Independents might have passed through the likely-voter screens used in the district surveys; the South, which has a lower proportion of Independents than the rest of the country, is under-represented in the district surveys; and marginal districts might have a higher proportion of Independents than safe districts. The incumbent advantage among Independents is comparable to that registered among partisan defectors.

A sizable number of voters cast their ballots for the U.S. House of Representatives without any guidance from party identification; the number of voters falling in this category varies substantially over congressional districts. Are their votes determined by public assessments of the candidates? The following analysis turns directly on this question.

Candidate Saliency and Vote Choice

For many years the ability of a voter to recall the name of one or both candidates was thought to be a prime determinant of partisan defection in congressional elections. Stokes and Miller first noted that deviations from party voting begin to appear when voters show some sign of knowing something about the opposition party's candidate. Table 4-3, taken from their analysis, demonstrates that defection increases as information about the opposition candidate relative to one's own candidate increases. Ferejohn, using name recall to measure candidate

55

Table 4-3
PARTY DEFECTION AND CANDIDATE AWARENESS IN CONTESTED DISTRICTS, 1958
(in percentages)

| | Voter Was Aware of: | | | |
Voted for:	Own party's candidate only	Neither candidate	Both candidates	Other party's candidate only
Own party's candidate	98	92	83	60
Other party's candidate	2	8	17	40
Total	100	100	100	100
N	(166)	(368)	(196)	(68)

Note: The survey question used in gathering the candidate-awareness data was: "Have you read or heard anything about (NAME OF CANDIDATE)?"
Source: Donald Stokes and Warren Miller, "Party Government and the Saliency of Congress," in *Elections and the Political Order*, p. 205.

saliency, found the same general pattern of relationships during the period 1958–1970, although he also noted a general increase in defection after 1958 (see Table 4-4).

Defection is least likely to occur among voters who know only their own party's candidate, most likely among those who know only the other party's candidate. Unfortunately, the number of voters who fall in the latter category is so small that very little defection is explained by this contrast in information about the candidates. In addition, voter awareness of the candidates offers no explanation whatsoever for the defection that still occurs among those who know only their own party's candidate or who know neither. And, what about those who know both? Candidate preference, not just awareness, must be a factor leading to defection.

Comparable figures for each of the ten 1976 DSG district surveys are summarized in Table 4-5. The overall pattern of relationships between candidate saliency and defection remains the same, although in four of the districts defection was higher among voters who recalled the name of neither candidate than among those who recalled the names of both. There is substantial variation in defection rates across districts within the information states, certainly more than expected from sampling error alone, which suggests that something other than simple candidate saliency leads voters to defect from their party's candidate.

The inadequacy of what Abramowitz called the name-familiarity

Table 4-4
PARTY DEFECTION, BY SALIENCY OF CANDIDATES IN CONTESTED DISTRICTS, SELECTED HOUSE ELECTIONS, 1958–1970

	Voter Recalled the Name of:			
Year	Own party's candidate only	Neither candidate	Both candidates	Other party's candidate only
1958	1	5	19	33
N	(134)	(290)	(221)	(30)
1964	5	14	21	40
N	(164)	(250)	(245)	(34)
1966	4	13	19	65
N	(96)	(193)	(163)	(15)
1968	5	18	23	51
N	(94)	(192)	(235)	(28)
1970	1	10	24	64
N	(110)	(185)	(107)	(16)

Note: Entries are percentages of all partisans in each name recall group who defected. Thus, 1 percent of the voters who recalled only the name of their own party's candidate defected to vote for the other party's candidate in 1958.
Source: John Ferejohn, "On the Decline of Competition in Congressional Elections," p. 173.

hypothesis for explaining partisan defection is even more apparent when the effects of both incumbency and saliency are examined. Table 4-6 captures the independent effects of incumbency and saliency on party voting. In every case, knowledge of the candidate increased his vote, although among incumbent partisans the differences were extremely small: 12 percent of the incumbent partisans who recalled the name of the challenger defected—and 11 percent of those who did not, also defected. (In fact, since knowledge of the challenger increased defection among incumbent partisans in only three of the ten districts, we must reject the saliency or name-familiarity hypothesis for this group. In each of the other three groups the results from seven or more districts out of the ten were consistent with the hypothesis.) The ability to recall the name of the candidates has a more marked effect among challenger partisans than among incumbent partisans. But the most striking observation to be made about the data in Table 4-6 is that

Table 4-5

PARTY DEFECTION, BY SALIENCY OF CANDIDATES, IN
TEN MARGINAL DISTRICTS, 1976

(in percentages)

| | Voter Recalled the Name of: | | | |
Party Defection	Own party's candidate only	Neither candidate	Both candidates	Other party's candidate only
Mean	7	19	21	46
Range	0 to 16	14 to 26	9 to 45	24 to 65

Source: DSG surveys.

the impact of incumbency is largely independent of saliency. The effects of incumbency on defection independent of saliency are three times greater than the effects of saliency alone.[6] One-fourth of the challenger partisans who did not recall the name of the incumbent nonetheless crossed party lines to support that incumbent, while only 11 percent of the incumbent partisans who did not recall the name of the challenger defected to that challenger. Incumbents lost 13 percent of their partisans who did not recall their names, challengers lost 35 percent.

To summarize, four patterns can be discerned in these defection rates. First, candidate saliency (measured here as name recall) accounts for some variation in defection rates. Incumbents gain more challenger partisans and lose fewer of their own partisans when voters recall their names than when they don't; challengers reduce defection among their own partisans when those partisans recall their names. Second, incumbents lose fewer of their own partisans and gain more of the opposition's partisans than equally salient challengers. Third, some defection can be attributed to neither saliency nor incumbency. Why, for example, do 11 percent of incumbent partisans support the challenger even though they cannot recall his name? Fourth, additional variation in defection rates can be seen once we move from mean values computed for the ten districts to the situation in individual districts. Since each of the four pairs of mean defection rates in Table 4-6 is based on ten districts, there are forty independent tests of both the saliency and

---

[6] Using the data in Table 4-6, the calculation for incumbency effects is as follows: $(25 - 9) + (35 - 13) + (36 - 12) + (25 - 11) = 76$ percentage points; for saliency effects, $(13 - 9) + (12 - 11) + (36 - 25) + (35 - 25) = 26$ percentage points.

Table 4-6
PARTY DEFECTION, BY INCUMBENCY AND SALIENCY OF CANDIDATES, IN TEN MARGINAL DISTRICTS, 1976

Voter Identified with:	Voter Recalled the Name of:			
	Incumbent		Challenger	
	Yes	No	Yes	No
Incumbent's party	9	13	12	11
Challenger's party	36	25	25	35

Note: Entries are mean percentages of the stated name recall and party-identification group who defected. Thus, 9 percent of the voters who recalled the name of the incumbent and identified with the incumbent's party defected to vote for the challenger.
Source: DSG surveys.

incumbency hypotheses. In thirteen of them, name recall did not increase the candidate's vote. In five of the forty cases the incumbent benefited less than his challenger. Moreover, the magnitude of the electoral benefit acruing to candidates because of saliency or incumbency varied considerably across districts.

These findings are not unexpected given the discussion in Chapter 3 of the limitations of name recall measures of candidate saliency. Many voters unable to recall the name of the candidate are able to recognize the name when they see it, and those who recognize a candidate's name do not invariably have a positive perception of him. Public visibility is important in a limiting sense; those challengers who fail to penetrate the public consciousness are at an enormous disadvantage vis-à-vis incumbents, who are generally recognized by almost all of their constituents. Visibility does not insure popularity, but it is an essential prerequisite. Voters who fail to *recognize* a challenger's name, as opposed to those who cannot recall it, invariably move disproportionately into the incumbent's camp. In our ten districts, six challengers (out of the twenty candidates) were not recognized by sizable numbers of voters; among those who did not recognize them, the challengers lost an average of 38 percent of their own partisans and gained only 4 percent of the incumbents' partisans, while among all voters (both partisans and Independents) they trailed the incumbents by forty-four percentage points. That these challengers did not lose the support of *every* voter who did not recognize their names suggests that other factors, such as party loyalty and negative assessments of the incumbent, are at work as well. Nevertheless, the strength of the relationship between candidate name recognition and vote choice is impressive.

Reputation and Vote Choice

Congressional elections might profitably be viewed as opportunities for voters to express their satisfaction or dissatisfaction with the incumbent congressman. In Chapter 3, I showed that almost all voters recognized the incumbent, that voters within the same district disagreed in their evaluations of his performance, and that assessments of incumbents varied substantially across districts. Moreover, these individual and district-level differences are not simply reflections of underlying partisan loyalty. Table 4-7 presents data that bear directly on this question.

The evidence is striking. An incumbent's ability to preserve the loyalty of his own partisans and to attract support from the challenger's partisans is directly related to these voters' evaluation of his performance in office. In addition, support for the challenger among Independents increases dramatically as the incumbent's job rating decreases. When voters have too little information with which to evaluate the performance of the incumbent, defection rates in the two partisan groups are roughly equal.

These data help clarify why incumbent name recall does not translate decisively into electoral support. Some voters who recall the

Table 4-7
PARTY DEFECTION AND CHALLENGER SUPPORT AMONG INDEPENDENTS, BY INCUMBENT JOB RATING, IN TEN MARGINAL DISTRICTS, 1976

Voter's Party Identification	Incumbent's Job Rating				
	Excellent	Pretty good	Only fair	Poor	Don't know
Incumbent's party	2	7	27	53	10
Challenger's party	77	50	15	4	12
Independents	1	10	40	74	25

Note: Entries are mean percentages of the stated job-rating and party-identification group who defected or, in the case of Independents, who voted for the challenger. Thus, 2 percent of the voters who rated the incumbent's job performance "excellent" and who identified with the incumbent's party defected to vote for the challenger.

Source: DSG surveys.

60

name of the incumbent are critical of the job he is doing; others who fail to recall his name still recognize it and approve of his performance in office. Vote choice, then, often turns directly on judgments made about the incumbent.

Incumbent job ratings have their sharpest effect at the extremes. An "excellent" rating virtually assures the incumbent support, whatever the partisanship of the voter; a "poor" rating means that the incumbent will lose almost all of his challenger's partisans, three-fourths of the Independents, and at least half of his own partisans. In reality, incumbents' job ratings tend to cluster in the middle range where the effect is present but diminished: a voter who thinks the incumbent is doing a "pretty good" job is still more likely to vote for the incumbent than for the challenger, but less so than one who rates the incumbent "excellent." Candidates seldom receive "excellent" ratings above 15 percent or "poor" ratings above 10 percent. Yet even shifts in the distribution of voters over the middle categories of job performance are likely to have significant electoral consequences. In so far as their actions can effect these ratings, candidates should take very seriously the importance of their campaign activities.

The relationship between incumbent job rating and vote choice among incumbent partisans and challenger partisans is not entirely symmetrical. While incumbents lose a certain percentage of their own partisans who give them negative ratings, they gain a higher percentage of the challenger's partisans who give them positive ratings. It appears that for some reason challengers are not able to exploit fully the electoral payoffs that might be expected to accrue to them when the incumbent they face is not thought to be doing a good job. This suggests that public perceptions of challengers are also relevant to vote choice.

There is another indicator of the electoral relevance of public perceptions of the challenger. The figures in Table 4-7 are arithmetic means computed from data in ten districts. While the relationship is consistent in all the districts (as the incumbent's job rating declines, incumbent-partisan defection increases, challenger-partisan defection decreases, and support for the challenger among Independents increases), the percentages vary across districts. In some cases the range is quite narrow. For example, an "excellent" rating among incumbent partisans and a "poor" rating among challenger partisans both lead to 0 percent defection in six of the ten districts. In others, the range is more extensive—incumbents lose between 8 and 41 percent of their own partisans who rate their performance as only "fair." One explanation for this variation is the standing of the challenger—voters are more likely to punish an incumbent for a poor performance if an attrac-

Table 4-8
PARTY DEFECTION AND VOTES OF INDEPENDENTS, BY CANDIDATE THERMOMETER RATINGS, IN TEN MARGINAL DISTRICTS, 1976

Voter's Party Identification	Incumbent			Challenger			
	Posi-tive	Neutral	Nega-tive	Posi-tive	Neutral	Nega-tive	Don't recog-nize
Incumbent's party	4	19	49	46	12	4	4
Challenger's party	68	25	11	10	37	65	38
Independents	7	28	70	16	58	86	50

Note: The entries are mean percentages of the stated candidate-reputation and party-identification group who defected or, in the case of Independents, who voted for the opponent of the stated candidate. Thus, 4 percent of the voters who gave the incumbent a positive rating on the candidate thermometer and who identified with the incumbent's party defected to vote for the challenger.
Source: DSG surveys.

tive alternative exists. In this case the voter's task is to "choose the preferred candidate" rather than to "accept or reject the incumbent."

In order to take account of the contribution of public perceptions of the challenger to vote choice, it is necessary to shift from performance measures to indicators of general reputation. The feeling thermometer, modified for use in telephone surveys, suits this purpose nicely. Table 4-8 presents the mean percentage of defection (and of opposition support among Independents) by feelings toward the incumbent and toward the challenger. (A "don't recognize" category is included only for challengers, since all incumbents were recognized by almost all respondents.)

The correlation between candidate reputation and vote choice is strong for both incumbents and challengers. The ability of both candidates to hold their own partisans and attract opposition partisans is dependent upon their reputation with the voters; a positive reputation is also critically important for minimizing the opponent's support among Independents. While the form of the relationship is the same for incumbents and challengers, the latter appear to be at a disadvantage on two counts. First, their penalty for low visibility is direct and severe. Challengers lose over a third of their own partisans who say they do not recognize the challenger's name and over a third of their own partisans who give the challenger a neutral rating. (The latter category probably includes respondents who have very little or no information about the challenger.) The number who fail to recognize the incumbent is insignificant and the number rating the incumbent "neutral" is a good deal less than that recorded for most challengers.

Second, the asymmetry noted above in connection with incumbent job ratings is especially pronounced here. This can be seen clearly in Table 4-8. When rated positively, incumbents lose only 4 percent of their own partisans and gain 68 percent of the challenger's partisans. Challengers rated positively, on the other hand, still lose 10 percent of their own partisans and gain only 46 percent of the incumbent's partisans. The same incumbent advantage can be found for every comparable pair of entries in Table 4-8, including those showing the behavior of Independents. Why? The answer probably lies in the nature of the alternative. It is possible that a number of voters who rate the challenger positively think even better of the incumbent; the reverse is less likely to occur in view of the lower visibility of the challenger, but it is possible. In order to deal adequately with this phenomenon, the analysis must include candidate *preferences*, not just individual candidate ratings.

Candidate Preference and Vote Choice

The Candidate-Preference Model. A simple model taken from the study of presidential elections is available for this purpose. Richard Brody states the "decision rules" as follows:

> (1) Voters who say they favor one candidate more than another are very likely—on the order of 95 percent—to vote for their favored candidate. This rule holds regardless of how much they favor their favorite or even whether their most favored candidate is rated unfavorably. Americans appear to distinguish the lesser of two evils or the greater of two goods and vote accordingly. (2) Voters who are neutral or indifferent toward the candidates, i.e. those voters who give the candidates the same favorability rating, tend to vote for the candidate of their party.[7]

These principles are summarized in schematic form in Table 4-9.

Some further elaboration is necessary before these decision rules can be applied to congressional elections. While in presidential elections almost all voters recognize both candidates, in congressional

---

[7] Richard A. Brody, "Communications," *American Political Science Review*, vol. 70 (September 1976), p. 924.

Table 4-9
CANDIDATE-PREFERENCE MODEL: PREDICTED VOTE, BY PARTY IDENTIFICATION AND CANDIDATE PREFERENCE

Candidate Preferred on Feeling Thermometer	Party Identification		
	Incumbent's party	Independents	Challenger's party
Incumbent	A Incumbent	B Incumbent	C Incumbent
None	D Incumbent	E Abstain	F Challenger
Challenger	G Challenger	H Challenger	I Challenger

Source: Author's adaptation of Richard Brody's decision rules (Brody, "Communications," p. 924).

races substantial numbers of voters fail to recognize some challengers. These "don't recognize" responses on the candidate thermometer are translated into candidate preferences as follows:

Candidate A	Candidate B	Preferred Candidate
Positive	Don't recognize	Candidate A
Neutral	Don't recognize	None
Negative	Don't recognize	Candidate B
Don't recognize	Don't recognize	None

In cases where one candidate is not recognized, feelings toward the other candidate are decisive. Thus, we expect a voter to support a candidate he doesn't recognize if his feelings toward the other candidate are negative. In effect, "don't recognize" responses are treated as neutral.

Finally, the modified feeling thermometer used in the telephone surveys is a blunt instrument compared with the original SRC/CPS thermometer. The measure used here allows only two positive and two negative scores while the SRC/CPS measure allows respondents to express continuous gradations of feeling *between 0 and 100*. The potential cost for the district surveys is increased measurement error: it is likely that preferences between candidates less decisive than those implied by the distance between 1 and 2 or 4 and 5 will be coded as neutral. Hence, candidate-preference measures in the district surveys are conservative: they classify some voters as neutral when they actually have a slight preference for one of the candidates. On the other hand, to err on the conservative side when dealing with congressional elections is not altogether bad. Voters are unlikely to draw fine distinctions between candidates when information levels are low, as they more often are in congressional than presidential elections. Moreover, the likelihood of the complementary error—seeing a preference when none in fact exists—is lessened with the simpler instrument.

Brody's scheme is useful in several ways. If the evidence corroborates it, I will have confirmed empirically the operation of candidate-preference decision rules in congressional as well as presidential elections. And any systematic departures from the predictions that are found can be scrutinized for clues about peculiar characteristics of congressional elections. In addition, this scheme provides a very straightforward reading of the relative importance of party identification and candidate preference in congressional voting decisions. Any candidate's total vote can be broken down into four categories: (1) party-line votes consistent with candidate preference, (2) votes from Independents and opposition partisans consistent with candidate preference, (3) party-line votes in conflict with a preference for the other party's candidate, and (4) all other possible combinations. These categories correspond with the lettered cells in Table 4-9 as follows:

Votes consistent with:	*Votes for Incumbent*	*Votes for Challenger*
1. Party identification and candidate preference	A	I
2. Candidate preference only	B,C	G,H
3. Party identification only	D,G	C,F
4. Neither	E,F,H,I	A,B,D,E

The letters in italics indicate votes inconsistent with Brody's model as schematized in Table 4-9. The incumbent's and challenger's supporting coalitions can be compared in these terms.

Testing the Model in One District. Before testing the model's fit in ten congressional districts, let us examine a single case. Table 4-10 contains preelection data on the intended congressional vote, by party identification and candidate preference, from a DSG survey conducted in a Midwestern urban district in 1976. In this race a senior Democratic incumbent faced the Republican challenger who had almost upset him in 1974. In this table, the nine boxes correspond to the nine lettered cells of Table 4-9. The entries in each box that are inconsistent

65

Table 4-10
VOTING INTENTIONS, BY PARTY IDENTIFICATION AND CANDIDATE PREFERENCE, IN ONE MARGINAL DISTRICT, 1976

Candidate Preferred on Feeling Thermometer and Intended Vote	Party Identification					
	Incumbent's party		Independents		Challenger's party	
	N	%	N	%	N	%
	A		B (52)		C	
Incumbent						
Incumbent	(101)	89	(27)	87	(25)	78
Challenger	(6)	5	(1)	3	(4)	13
Undecided	(6)	5	(3)	10	(3)	9
	D		E		F	
None						
Incumbent	(21)	58	(3)	38	(5)	20
Challenger	(4)	11	(2)	24	(8)	32
Undecided	(11)	31	(3)	38	(12)	48
	G		H		I	
Challenger						
Incumbent	(8)	20	(2)	8	(5)	8
Challenger	(28)	70	(21)	81	(57)	90
Undecided	(4)	10	(3)	11	(1)	2

Note: Italics indicate outcomes inconsistent with the predictions of the candidate-preference model schematized in Table 4-9. The party-identification and candidate-preference boxes are lettered in the same way as the cells in Table 4-9.
Source: DSG survey.

with the outcome predicted by Table 4-9 are in italics. Thus, the model predicts that the incumbent will win all of the votes in cell A; in fact, in this district 5 percent of the votes in this cell went to the challenger. Similarly, in cell G, where the challenger was predicted to win, the 20 percent of the vote that went to the incumbent is in italics.

To see how well the model fits this district, we must examine each of the cells in this way. In every case, most of the votes are consistent with the predicted outcome. The 20 percent deviation in cell G is, in fact, the largest in the table; for one-fifth of the incumbent's partisans who preferred the challenger, party identification was strong enough to override candidate preference.

Adding up all of the italicized figures, we discover that 35 of the 366 predicted votes, or 10 percent, are "in error." The fit is good, although less so than for presidential elections. The percentage of votes inconsistent with the model is lowest when a candidate is preferred by his own partisans and Independents, highest when voters are neutral or indifferent toward the candidates or when partisanship conflicts with candidate preference. Undecided voters are concentrated among those who have no clear candidate preference.

It is interesting to note that the use of candidate preferences in this analysis, rather than separate candidate ratings, gives us a much clearer picture. In this particular district, for example, 52 percent of the incumbent partisans who gave the challenger a positive rating defected to the challenger,[8] but, as cell G in Table 4-10 shows, 70 percent of the incumbent's partisans who *preferred* the challenger did so. Most of the incumbent advantage seen in Table 4-8 is not present in Table 4-10. This can be seen clearly by comparing the number of votes inconsistent with the predicted vote in the appropriate pairs of cells (A and I, B and H, C and G, and D and F). In each case the deviations favor the incumbent, but the overall advantage is insignificant: 5.5 percent of all votes are deviations favoring the incumbent; 4.1 percent favor the challenger. The incumbent's advantage can be explained almost entirely on the basis of candidate preference.

The relative importance to each candidate of party identification and candidate preference can also be determined from the data in Table 4-10. Breaking down each candidate's votes into the four categories outlined above, we obtain the following:

	Incumbent		Challenger	
Votes consistent with:	N	%	N	%
1. Party identification and candidate preference	(101)	51	(57)	44
2. Candidate preference only	(52)	27	(49)	37
3. Party identification only	(29)	15	(12)	9
4. Neither	(15)	7	(13)	10
Total	(197)	100	(131)	100

Perhaps the most striking figures are those indicating the percentage of each candidate's support that comes from party identification independent of candidate preference. Only a small fraction of each candidate's votes (15 percent for the incumbent and 9 percent for the chal-

---

[8] DSG survey. This figure is one of those used in the computation of mean defection in Table 4-8.

lenger) falls in this category; virtually all of the party-line votes were cast by voters who rated their party's candidate higher than his opponent without regard to party. (Recall that feeling thermometer ratings were obtained without reference to the candidate's party or position.) In this district there was very little automatic party support; each candidate earned the votes of his own partisans by being perceived as the more desirable alternative. Of course, the voters' candidate preferences might very well have been influenced by their partisan views of the world, but the point here is that independent judgments were made.

A sizable part of each candidate's support was based on candidate preference alone (27 percent for the incumbent, 37 percent for the challenger); over a third of the challenger's votes came from Independents and incumbent partisans who preferred him to the incumbent. Candidate preference played a part in 78 percent of the incumbent's votes and 81 percent of the challenger's. One is tempted to conclude that the public's assessment of the candidates is a major factor in congressional voting. But the evidence thus far has been limited to a single district. Are these findings applicable to the other nine districts under investigation here?

Testing the Model in Ten Districts. The accuracy of the candidate-preference model in predicting individual votes in all ten congressional districts is set forth in Table 4-11, which summarizes the results of this kind of analysis for each of the districts. The mean percentage of votes inconsistent with the predictions increases steadily as one moves through the four party-identification and candidate-preference categories. The rate of deviation from the model is higher for challengers than incumbents, although this difference is significant in size and consistent across all districts only among partisans who are neutral toward the candidates and when party identification and candidate preference conflict. In the latter case, incumbents appear to have a slight edge over challengers in retaining the support of their own partisans who indicate a preference for the opponent. But since the number of cases falling in these two categories is quite small and since for the majority of voters candidate preference overrides partisanship, it is probably unwise to make too much of this difference. In the case of partisans who do not prefer one candidate, incumbents benefit from the challengers' lack of recognition. Some of the challenger partisans who say they are neutral toward the candidates may actually recognize only the incumbent and as a result defect to vote for the incumbent's party.

Almost all of the advantage of incumbents over challengers can be attributed to candidate preference. The 10 percent of all votes that

Table 4-11
PERFORMANCE OF CANDIDATE-PREFERENCE MODEL IN TEN CONGRESSIONAL DISTRICTS, 1976
(in percentages; "advantage" figures in percentage points)

Voter Category and Vote Predicted by the Model	Votes Deviating from Model	
	Mean	Range
Party identification and candidate preference coincide		
Incumbent (cell A)	2	0 to 5
Challenger (cell I)	8	0 to 24
Independents, one candidate preferred		
Incumbent (cell B)	6	0 to 15
Challenger (cell H)	13	0 to 36
Partisans, no candidate preferred		
Incumbent (cell D)	10	4 to 17
Challenger (cell F)	22	14 to 31
Party identification and candidate preference conflict		
Incumbent (cell C)	16	0 to 46
Challenger (cell G)	30	0 to 75
All votes	10	5 to 15
Total deviation favoring incumbent	6	3 to 10
Total deviation favoring challenger	4	2 to 8
Incumbent advantage	2	−1 to 4

Note: This table compares the relationships among party-identification, candidate-preference, and intended-vote in ten districts with the patterns predicted by the candidate-preference model schematized in Table 4-9. The table should be read as follows: Among voters whose party identification and candidate preference coincided and who were predicted by the candidate-preference model to vote for the incumbent (cell A in Table 4-9), a mean of 2 percent in the ten districts voted for the challengers. This figure ranged from 0 to 5 percent across the ten districts.

Source: Author's analysis of DSG surveys.

deviate from the model divides almost evenly: 6 percent favor the incumbent and 4 percent favor the challenger.

The range in the percentage of error in individual cells across districts is due to several factors. Some of the estimates are unstable because of the small number of cases: one or two votes can sometimes have a noticeable impact on these figures. In several cases the enormous size of the range is due almost entirely to a single district. The removal of just one district from each of the following cells lowers the upper limit substantially: in cell I the range drops from twenty-four to ten percentage points, in cell C from forty-six to twenty-one percentage points, in cell G from seventy-five to forty-seven percentage points, in cell H from thirty-six to seventeen percentage points. The explanations for these anomalous cases must go beyond party and candidate preference. In one Southern district, for example, a former incumbent held many of his own partisans who rated the incumbent higher; and in another Southern district an incumbent retained the support of her own partisans who rated the challenger, another former incumbent, higher. In both cases the fact that partisanship proved a match for candidate preference may well have been a result of presidential coattails.

The contribution to each candidate's total vote of party identification and candidate preference is summarized in Table 4-12. It corroborates many of the conclusions reached for the single district analyzed above. Routine party support not backed up by express preference for the party's candidate provides a very small part of each candidate's total support, although it is more important to challengers than to incumbents. This is especially true for challengers with low visibility, who generate so little personal support that the independent contribution of party identification is three to five times more important than that of candidate preference. Incumbents are generally more successful in conveying a favorable image (at least one more favorable than the challenger's) to Independents and opposition partisans.

Differences between the incumbent and challenger in the composition of their support reveal a good deal about the nature of the contest in specific districts. Some incumbents are spared defeat at the hands of visible and popular challengers by a favorable division of partisans in their district; other incumbents forge supporting coalitions on the basis of personal appeal in the face of an unfavorable division of partisans. Some challengers mount formidable campaigns that reach well beyond their own partisan base; others fail to achieve the recognition that is a prerequisite for making inroads among Independents and incumbent partisans. Whatever the particular combination of strengths and weaknesses, all candidates derive the vast majority of their support from voters who express a clear preference for them as individuals.

In summary, the evidence supports the view that public evaluations of the candidates are very important in congressional as well as presidential elections. Most party-line votes are accompanied by a favorable perception of the party's candidate; when partisanship and candidate preference conflict, voters are likely to defect from their party. Incumbents have an advantage over challengers primarily because the public usually sees them as the more attractive alternative. But an incumbent's ability to attract favorable ratings from his con-

Table 4-12

CONTRIBUTION OF PARTY IDENTIFICATION AND CANDIDATE PREFERENCE TO EACH CANDIDATE'S TOTAL VOTE IN TEN CONGRESSIONAL DISTRICTS, 1976

Percentage of Each Candidate's Total Vote Consistent with:	Incumbent		Challenger	
	Mean	Range	Mean	Range
Party identification and candidate preference	45	28 to 63	44	22 to 54
Candidate preference only	27	11 to 40	21	6 to 39
Party identification only	14	10 to 20	23	11 to 41
Neither	13	3 to 26	13	7 to 25

Source: DSG surveys.

stituents and the challenger's effectiveness in becoming known and liked together directly influence the size of that advantage.

Some Thoughts on the Development of Candidate Images

If votes for Congress are determined primarily by the reputations of the candidates, it is important to explore the bases of the candidate images held by the public. Is it possible to generalize about the factors that lead voters to like or dislike incumbents and challengers? For example, can one point to certain types of activities of incumbents or to issues as determinants of public attitudes toward the candidates that might bias the system in favor of incumbents?

There is little systematic evidence that directly links the activities of incumbents in office with their reputation among their constituents. Mayhew presents a very compelling argument that desire for reelection fuels congressmen's drive for advertising, credit-taking, and position-taking, all of which consume enormous chunks of their time and resources and which convey to the voters a uniformly positive impression of the incumbent.[9] Cover's attempt to measure one element of incumbent activity—frequency of press releases and mass mailings—and relate it to the saliency of the incumbent was not very successful, but this failure to find a strong empirical connection probably has much to do with the inadequacy of the measures.[10]

---

[9] Mayhew, *Congress: The Electoral Connection*, chap. 1.
[10] For example, Cover's dependent variable was name recall, not recognition or reputation. Cover, "Advantage," chap. 3.

Fiorina concentrates on one of Mayhew's categories—credit-taking or the ombudsman role.[11] He argues that the advantage of incumbency increased during the 1960s because congressmen became less oriented to partisan and controversial legislative work and national policy making and more consumed with nonpartisan, noncontroversial, errand-boy activities. The rise of the Washington bureaucracy provided congressmen with increased opportunities to help the folks back home, which in turn led to increased electoral support. There are several problems with Fiorina's analysis. First, it neglects for no compelling reason those communications or contacts with constituents unrelated to ombudsman activities. Second, no evidence is available to link these ombudsman activities with changes in public attitudes. And third, the hypothesized shift in legislative role orientation does not square with reality. Newer members of Congress are more issue-oriented than their predecessors and seem to invest a higher proportion of their staff resources in legislative activities. Changes in the structure of decision making in the House of Representatives have facilitated increased legislative activity, both in committee and on the floor, among junior members. At the same time, however, these congressmen have proven themselves very resourceful in devising new modes of communication with their constituents, from mobile offices to town meetings to work days, all of which tend to generate favorable publicity for them.

Little systematic evidence is available on how members' contact with their constituents influences public attitudes and votes. However, two pieces of information relevant to this discussion are available from the candidate surveys. In one district represented by an incumbent for twenty years, those voters who said they had received "personal help or communication" from their congressman (about a fourth of all the voters in the district) were no more likely to vote for him than those that had not. In another district, represented by a freshman member who, as a challenger, had devised the work day as a campaign technique and continued using it once elected, almost a fifth of the voters mentioned that their congressman was "out with the people" or something comparable in response to the open-ended question, "What did you like most about Congressman X?" In the first example, casework and personal correspondence had no measurable electoral payoff, perhaps partly because these activities were neutralized by other more dramatic aspects of both candidates' public images. In the second example, the incumbent benefited from his constituency contacts, but

---

[11] Morris P. Fiorina, *Congress: Keystone of the Washington Establishment* (New Haven: Yale University Press, 1977).

these did not actually depend upon resources that accrued to him as an incumbent.

Incumbents have available numerous resources with which to present themselves in a favorable light to their constituents. In the absence of other communication about the incumbent, this generalized favorable image can have decisive electoral effects. But publicly perceived candidate images can also reflect the political dialogue in the district. Charges of impropriety, insensitivity, incompetence, or ineffectiveness, if plausible and forcefully made in the context of an attractive alternative, can override the incumbent's advantages in communication. It is up to the challenger to find grounds for such charges and to mount a campaign that makes them known.

Does a candidate's position on an issue ever constitute the basis for public dissatisfaction? In the last chapter I discussed some of the reasons why policy or issue voting was not prevalent in congressional elections. However, as Fiorina, Kingdon, and others have argued, issues can hurt candidates without the requirements of policy voting being fully satisfied. A candidate can lose support because of his position on an issue either indirectly, when attentive elites convey to others their unhappiness with the candidate, or directly, when the issue is sufficiently salient to arouse public discontent. A dramatic instance of the latter occurred in 1974 when a Republican member of the House Judiciary Committee outspokenly defended President Nixon during the nationally televised Watergate hearings. In this case the general public was attentive: two-thirds of the district's voters watched the hearings and were aware of their congressman's position on impeachment. The committee was given a 59 percent favorable rating, while the incumbent's performance on the committee earned him only a 35 percent favorable rating. By a margin of 51 to 39 percent, the voters disapproved of the congressman's support of President Nixon; even two-fifths of the Republicans in the district disapproved. These negative feelings toward the incumbent translated very directly into electoral support for his opponent.

Of course, seldom is a candidate's position on an issue conveyed so vividly to the electorate. More typically, smaller numbers of voters become aware of a candidate's stance when it conflicts with their own strongly held beliefs. For example, in a Western district in which public sentiment runs very strongly against any form of gun control, a Democratic candidate's tentative and lukewarm opposition to gun control presented his opponent with an opportunity to characterize the Democrat as pro–gun control. The local media gave some attention to the Democrat's initial statement, his opponent's charges, and subsequent clarifications and denials. When the dust settled, 13 percent of

73

the voters thought the Democrat favored gun control, 19 percent thought he opposed it, and 68 percent did not know what his position on gun control was. However, even though most voters remained unaware of his position and more thought he opposed gun control than thought he favored it, some electoral damage was done. Most of those voters who perceived the Democrat as favoring gun control themselves strongly opposed it, and they intended to vote for his opponent; this group of voters included Democrats and Independents as well as Republicans.

Issues are seldom offered by voters as reasons for liking or supporting congressional candidates; they are much more likely to surface in a negative context. Candidates must continuously articulate positions on issues to satisfy groups within their constitutencies and to demonstrate competence and sensitivity. But public awareness of a candidate's position on a particular issue remains low unless that position is dramatically out of step with opinion in the district. In order to preserve a favorable public image, incumbents must act to forestall criticism on policy grounds. Success in this regard assures continued public ignorance of their positions, but it also provides a form of accountability to district sentiment.[12]

If public knowledge of a candidate's position on specific issues is extremely limited, perceptions of general ideological stances are somewhat more common. The prevalence and accuracy of these perceptions were reviewed in the last chapter; here I want to investigate the electoral implications of ideological distance. Table 4-13 presents the appropriate data from six congressional districts.[13] As it shows, incumbent partisans are more likely to defect if they perceive the challenger to be closer to them ideologically than the incumbent; similarly, challenger partisans who see the incumbent as closer to their own position defect at a rate over three times that of those who perceive the challenger to be closer ideologically. While these mean scores are striking, the real electoral penalty for ideological distance is limited by the number of voters who fall in the critical cells. The percentage of the electorate able to describe the general ideological stance of the two candidates and themselves ranged from 26 percent to 58 percent in the six districts considered here. Since the number of partisans who perceived the other party candidate as closer never exceeded 7 percent of the electorate, the shift in votes due to ideological proximity was only three percentage points or less. Of course, in a close election

---

[12] For supporting arguments and evidence, see Kingdon, *Congressmen's Voting Decisions*, chap. 2; and Warren E. Miller and Donald E. Stokes, "Constituency Influence in Congress," in *Elections and the Political Order*, pp. 369–370.

[13] These were the only districts for which the necessary measures were available.

Table 4-13

PARTY DEFECTION, BY IDEOLOGICAL DISTANCE, IN SIX MARGINAL DISTRICTS, 1976

(in percentages)

Voter's Party Identification	Voter's Ideological Position		
	Close to incumbent	Equidistant from candidates	Close to challenger
Incumbent's party	11	15	36
Challenger's party	49	31	15

Note: Entries are percentages of the stated ideological and party-identification group who defected. Thus 11 percent of the voters who thought their ideological position was close to the incumbent's and who identified with the incumbent's party defected to vote for the challenger.
Source: DSG surveys.

these votes could mean the difference between victory and defeat. Moreover, candidates no doubt realize that electoral costs increase as public perceptions of ideological distance increase.

Quite apart from the activities of incumbents and the role of issues, candidate images can develop as a result of political communication generated by the campaign itself. While a full investigation of the effects of campaign activities on public attitudes toward the candidates is beyond the scope of this study, it is possible to explore some general patterns of change in public support for the candidates in the year preceding the election and the ways in which actions by the candidates themselves influence the direction and magnitude of these changes.

Changes over Time

Earlier in this chapter I discussed changes in the support for incumbents and challengers between the final preelection survey and the election. Here I want to concentrate on changes occurring prior to and during the campaign that can be measured directly, with surveys taken in the same district at several points in time.

The typical pattern of change in support for incumbents and challengers found in these districts would not surprise most analysts of congressional elections. Even in presumably marginal districts, most incumbents amass an early lead over their challengers based on an overwhelming advantage in public visibility; this lead narrows as the challenger's candidacy begins to penetrate the electorate's consciousness, but it is usually sufficiently large to insure victory in November. There are several important variations on this pattern. The magnitude of the early lead depends most directly on the visibility and reputation of the candidates. In districts with comparable distributions of partisans, well before the election some incumbents receive positive job ratings fifteen to twenty percentage points higher than others, leading to substantial differences in the size of the early lead. The potential vulnerability of an incumbent can often be assessed with an early reading of public opinion in his district; the telltale signs are mediocre job-approval scores and absolute levels of voter preference of less than 50 percent. In these cases the electoral fate of the incumbent depends in large part upon the ability of the challenger to present a publicly visible and attractive alternative.

In addition to differences in the magnitude of their lead, incumbents vary in terms of the time of their greatest strength. Most incumbents, particularly senior ones, attract fairly constant levels of support that change only in the heat of a campaign, if at all. With others, including some freshmen members, there are noticeable surges in support that appear to result at least partially from intensive public relations efforts such as more frequent mass mailings and press coverage of constituency activities.[14] So while some incumbents enjoy a high plateau of support throughout the congressional term, others achieve a peak just prior to the onset of the campaign. In both cases, however, their advantage over the challenger subsequently narrows.

In districts where the challenger is well known prior to the active phase of the campaign, some other pattern of change is more likely to occur. Without the inflated advantage due to low challenger visibility, incumbents begin in a position closer to their true electoral strength and need not lose ground as election day approaches. In some cases the incumbent actually widens his lead over the challenger (or captures the lead he never had) as a result of actions taken during the campaign.

Several examples illustrate these patterns. The first involves a large, primarily rural farm district in the Midwest, whose politics had been controlled by the Republicans for many years. By the early 1970s the partisan division in the district represented by the identifications of its individual voters was essentially even, although the senior Republican congressman continued to enjoy wide margins at the polls. In 1972 an aggressive and well-financed challenge netted the Democrats almost 45 percent. The same Democratic candidate filed for the seat in 1974, but a survey in June of that year found him far behind the

---

[14] The basis for this generalization consists largely of information on incumbent activity and mass opinion in two congressional districts.

Republican incumbent (56 percent to 27 percent). By October his lead had shrunk to six percentage points, largely as a result of the increasing visibility and popularity of the challenger, though partly as a consequence of a cooling of feelings toward the incumbent. This momentum continued, and the challenger won the election with 51 percent of the vote. Less than a year and a half into his first term, following extensive use of work days, a mobile office, town meetings, and district newsletters, this Democrat enjoyed very high approval among his constituents and led the likely Republican opponent by a margin of 69 percent to 15 percent. By September his lead had narrowed slightly: 64 percent to 19 percent. In November the incumbent won with 65 percent of the total vote.

While many observations could be made about the recent electoral history of this district, for our purposes, two are germane. First, the incumbents' early leads were inflated; they declined as the challengers became better known and began to attract their own natural supporters. Second, the enormous Democratic swing in this district between 1974 and 1976 cannot simply be attributed to the advantage of incumbency. The ability of this Democratic incumbent to generate support well beyond the norm for his colleagues in the class of 1974 and the failure of the Republican challenger to make a substantial impression among the voters (as his opponent had done in a comparable situation four years earlier) were important factors in this electoral shift.

The electoral situation confronting another Democratic freshman was quite different. Halfway into his first term, he trailed his likely Republican opponent by eleven percentage points; during the next twelve months he gradually recaptured the lead and ultimately won the election with 54 percent of the vote (see Table 4-14). The district, like a number of others in the South, had returned its Republican representative to Congress in 1970 and 1972 by wide margins in spite of the overwhelmingly Democratic identifications of its voters. However, in 1974 the strong national tides favoring the Democratic party were especially pronounced in the state, touching every race from county sheriff to U.S. senator. The incumbent suffered a drop of seventeen percentage points from his 1972 vote and was defeated. Yet twelve months later he still enjoyed a considerable advantage in public reputation over the victorious Democrat. As the Democrat finally began to exploit the channels of political communication at his disposal, that advantage lessened and ultimately disappeared. The election was decided during the active phase of the campaign when most voters had distinct views of both candidates.

Another example is drawn from a farm belt district whose partisan loyalties are evenly divided between the two parties, largely because

Table 4-14

CHANGES IN CANDIDATE STRENGTH IN A SOUTHERN DISTRICT, NOVEMBER 1975–OCTOBER 1976

(in percentages)

	Date of Survey			
Candidate and Measure	Nov. 1975	May 1976	Sept. 1976	Oct. 1976
Democrat (first-term incumbent)				
Name recall	41	51	54	60
Name recognition	85	86	93	94
Positive thermometer	32	35	37	42
Negative thermometer	14	15	18	21
Favorable job rating	41	44	54	—
Republican (former incumbent)				
Name recall	—	—	37	59
Name recognition	96	93	95	96
Positive thermometer	50	42	38	33
Negative thermometer	21	24	25	31
Vote Intention				
Democrat	39	41	42	46
Republican	50	44	44	41
Undecided	11	15	14	13

Source: DSG surveys.

of the Democratic base in the one substantial city situated within its boundaries. For many years the Republican incumbent was accustomed to receiving at least two-thirds of the votes cast for Congress, but in 1974 his margin slipped dramatically to seven percentage points. In 1976 he faced a new Democratic challenger, someone active in city school board politics but without district-wide exposure. Following the Democratic primary, an August survey showed the incumbent leading by a margin of 50 percent to 35 percent. During the next two months, while measures of the incumbent's reputation remained constant, the challenger gained in visibility (his name recall increased from 26 to 63 percent) and reputation. Three weeks before the election the margin had narrowed to eleven percentage points. This trend accelerated, and the challenger won with just over 50 percent of the vote.

A final example illustrates the point that while incumbents, particularly senior incumbents, have a very difficult time changing public attitudes toward themselves during the short span of a campaign, they can decisively alter the outcome of the race by influencing public attitudes toward their opponent. This case is drawn from a Midwestern urban district represented for many years by a Democrat, whose safe margins abruptly turned competitive in 1974 following his arrest for drunken driving. Paired against the same Republican challenger he had faced in 1974, the incumbent held only a five percentage point lead in August 1976 (46 percent to 41 percent), in spite of a large advantage in name recognition. At this stage the evidence pointed to a sizable Republican victory in November. A decision was made to launch a strong attack on the personal stability and qualifications of the challenger, an attack articulated not by the incumbent but by a consortium of labor unions. A good deal of media attention was given to the charges and to the challenger's response. By early October the damage was registered in public attitudes toward the challenger. While the percentage of the electorate able to recall the challenger's name had increased by twenty percentage points, the proportion viewing the challenger negatively had also increased from a third to half. Voters now expressed a 52 percent to 34 percent preference for the Democratic incumbent, who a month later won reelection with 54 percent of the vote.

As I indicated at the beginning of this section, the outcomes of most congressional elections are determined well before the onset of active campaigning. Incumbents typically enjoy an enormous advantage in visibility and reputation many months before the election, and the efforts of most challengers to close the gap are inadequate. But this does not mean that incumbency is invincible or that campaigns are irrelevant. As we have seen in the examples above, public attitudes toward the candidate reflect the extent and nature of political communication generated by those candidates. Some decisive change now occurs during campaigns, and the potential for more is surely there.

5

Candidates and Election Outcomes

Individual voting in congressional elections is clearly responsive to perceptions of the candidates. The evidence presented in earlier chapters demonstrates that a very large part of the public in a sample of districts is aware of congressional candidates and votes for the preferred candidate. Incumbents have a clear advantage over challengers in visibility and reputation, but to be known is not necessarily to be liked. There is sufficient variation in candidate reputations independent of party loyalty to suggest that candidates have much to do with their own electoral fates.

The investigation to this point has focused primarily on the individual voter, albeit the individual voter in a number of congressional districts. Does the importance of public knowledge of the candidates look equally compelling when the unit of analysis switches from the individual voter to the congressional district? My plan in this chapter is to examine the 1974 and 1976 election returns in the districts for which some public opinion information is available and to determine whether these electoral *outcomes* reflect the relative visibility and reputation of the candidates.

In Chapter 2, I argued that the appropriateness of various explanations of behavior in congressional elections was dependent upon the level of analysis (the nation, the district, the individual) and on the relative emphasis on continuity and change. I also pointed out that the vantage point of most candidates brings into sharpest relief those factors that depend on the candidate himself. National forces are certainly present, but the swing across districts is far from uniform: local factors such as candidates, issues, and district influences on national forces must have some bearing on electoral change at the district level. We can judge the accuracy of these observations by examining the 1974 and 1976 congressional election returns.

Perspectives on the 1974 and 1976 Congressional Elections

On its face the national outcome of the 1974 congressional elections seemed to be at odds with the overwhelming evidence that incumbent congressmen were becoming increasingly invulnerable to electoral defeat. The 1972–1974 national swing in the popular vote for the two major parties—six percentage points Democratic—was matched by a net swing of forty-eight seats Democratic in the House of Representatives, a vote/seat ratio not very different from those recorded earlier in the century. Forty incumbents were defeated in the general election (another eight in the primaries) and a total of ninety-two new members, comprising over a fifth of the House, were elected to the 94th Congress.

The 1976 elections fit more easily into the pattern of recent elections. Only two of the freshmen members seeking reelection were defeated, even though many represented districts traditionally held by the other party; and one of these losses can be attributed to adverse publicity surrounding the incumbent's arrest and conviction for sex solicitation. A total of twelve incumbents lost in the general elections, and the national popular vote swing of 1.6 percentage points Republican produced no net gain in seats; in fact, the Democrats actually gained one seat over their 1974 total, two over the number they held just prior to the 1976 election. A high retirement rate was largely responsible for the election of sixty-nine new members to the 95th Congress.

In their underlying structure, these elections are similar to those described by David Mayhew: open-seat districts cluster in the marginal range while districts with incumbents running peak in three places—relatively safe Republican, safe Democratic, and uncontested Democratic.[1] There is no evidence that the 1974 elections reversed the trend toward vanishing marginals; the sizable swing in the national popular vote shifted the safe Republican mode at least partly into the marginal range, but the number of districts falling in this range has not noticeably increased.

Yet the fact remains that a large number of Republican incumbents were defeated in 1974, substantially more than a six percentage point vote swing should have produced, given the 1972 distribution of marginal Republican districts. Had the 1972–1974 swing been uniform across all districts, the twenty-nine Republican incumbents seeking reelection in 1974 who won their 1972 races with less than

---

[1] Mayhew, "Congressional Elections: The Case of the Vanishing Marginals," pp. 298–302.

56 percent of the vote would have all been defeated. In fact fifteen of these precariously marginal incumbents survived while many of their colleagues who had attracted 60 percent or more of the vote in 1972 were defeated. (The thirty-six Republican incumbents defeated in 1974 had 1972 vote totals that divided evenly into three categories: less than 55 percent; 55 to 60 percent; more than 60 percent.) Electoral change at the level of the congressional district in 1974 was highly variable, and predictions about the magnitude and location of seat turnover based only on the structure of competition and the size of the national popular vote swing would have been extremely inaccurate.

Upon closer inspection, the 1976 election also reveals important variability in swing at the district level. Some seats changed party hands with swings well in excess of the national swing; in hotly contested seats where the winner's margin was five percentage points or less, substantially more Democrats than Republicans were successful, in both open seats and incumbent-contested seats. The absence of a strong national tide in 1976 precludes another test of the impact of the structure of competition on the vote/seat relationship—and directs our attention to local determinants of the electoral change that did occur.

The heterogeneity of partisan swing can be seen most readily from the data in Figure 5-1, which presents the distribution of swing across districts in the 1974 and 1976 elections. The figure represents the change in the vote between 1972 and 1974 and between 1974 and 1976 in every congressional district contested by both major parties. If change were induced primarily by national forces, we would expect virtually all of the districts to cluster around the national swing— that is, to have roughly the same change in the vote. Instead, the most notable characteristic of both distributions is the wide dispersion about the mean. The 1972–1974 swing ranges from a 28.0 percentage point gain for the Republicans to a 36.2 percentage point gain for the Democrats; the 1974–1976 range is even greater—38.0 percentage points Republican to 31.6 percentage points Democratic. These ranges cannot be dismissed as the result of several atypical cases; the wide dispersion can be seen from the standard deviation for each distribution: 9.6 percentage points in 1972–1974 and 9.0 percentage points in 1974–1976. So, for example, in 1972–1974 about a fifth of all congressional districts experienced swings in favor of the Republican party while another fifth registered swings toward the Democrats in excess of 15 percentage points. Knowing that the national popular vote swing was 6.0 percentage points does not provide a very reliable guide to electoral change in individual districts.

Figure 5-1

DISTRIBUTION OF PARTISAN SWING IN CONGRESSIONAL ELECTIONS, 1972–1974 AND 1974–1976

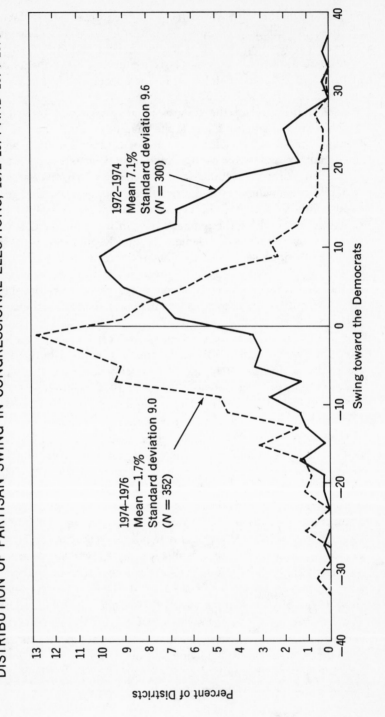

Table 5-1
DISTRIBUTION OF SWING IN BRITISH AND U.S. CONSTITUENCIES, SELECTED YEARS, 1862–1976

Election	Standard Deviation	Variance
Britain		
1892–1895	3.0	9.0
1959–1964	2.4	5.8
1966–1970	2.6	6.8
United States		
1862–1864[a]	4.7	22.2
1956–1958	5.5	30.3
1958–1960	5.6	31.4
1972–1974	9.6	92.2
1974–1976	9.0	81.0

[a] Excludes Southern districts.

Source: Figures for the two most recent U.S. swings were computed by the author. The others are taken from Stokes, "Parties and the Nationalization of Political Forces," p. 192, and Burnham, "Insulation and Responsiveness in Congressional Elections," p. 421.

The lack of uniformity in recent partisan swings is dramatized by a comparison with swing figures from Britain. Table 5-1 contains the standard deviation and variance in swing across British and U.S. constituencies for pairs of elections in the distant and recent past. The contrast between the two countries, which Donald Stokes noted some years ago, is striking: Britain comes much closer than the United States to a uniform national swing, suggesting that political change in Britain is largely a consequence of the electorate's response to national concerns. But also striking is the change that has occurred within the United States over the last decade and a half: between 1956–1958 and 1972–1974 the variance in swing tripled.

Most scholars would no doubt attribute this increase in the variance—a localization of political change—to the increasing advantage of incumbency. There is some evidence that incumbency contributes to the variability of swing. David Mayhew and Albert Cover have noted two kinds of contests whose results systematically depart from the national swing.[2] The first are open seats, in which the party of

[2] The most recent use of these concepts by the authors is found in their "Congressional Dynamics and the Decline of Competitive Congressional Elections," pp. 59–60.

Table 5-2

DROP IN SUPPORT FOR THE INCUMBENT'S PARTY WHEN INCUMBENT RETIRES, 1972–1974 AND 1974–1976 ("RETIREMENT SLUMP")

(in percentage points)

Party of Retiring Incumbent	1972–1974			1974–1976		
	Mean	Range	N	Mean	Range	N
Actual change						
Democrat	+1.2	−13.4 to +16.4	(21)	−5.2	−30.8 to +27.5	(26)
Republican	−11.8	−26.0 to + 0.6	(23)	−8.7	−31.6 to + 6.8	(15)
Adjusted for national swing[a]						
Democrat	−4.8	−18.4 to +10.4		−3.6	−29.2 to +29.1	
Republican	−5.8	−20.0 to + 6.6		−10.3	−33.2 to + 5.2	
All districts with retiring incumbent	−5.3	−20.0 to +10.4	(44)	−6.0	−33.2 to +29.1	(41)

[a] The national popular vote swing was 6.0 percentage points Democratic in 1972–1974 and 1.6 percentage points Republican in 1974–1976.

Source: The definition for "retirement slump" is taken from Cover, "Advangage," p. 19. Author's calculations from official election returns.

the retiring incumbent usually attracts considerably less support than it last did when the incumbent was its nominee. The second are seats in which freshmen members are seeking their first reelection; in these contests, freshmen of both parties usually run well ahead of the national tide. "Retirement slump" is the effect of removing the incumbency advantage; "sophomore surge" is the electoral reward of running as a first-term incumbent. Figures from both kinds of contests for 1972–1974 and 1974–1976 are presented in Tables 5-2 and 5-3.

The mean scores are in line with those reported for earlier years by Mayhew and Cover. When they are adjusted for national partisan swing, we see that the successor of the average retiring incumbent in 1974 ran 5.3 percentage points behind the incumbent's last showing; in 1976 the slump was 6.0 percentage points. Similarly in 1974 freshmen members gained on the average of 5.8 percentage points over their first showing; in 1976 the surge was 6.8 percentage points. There is no question that *on the average* a party's support declined following the retirement of its incumbent, and support for freshmen of both parties increased in their first reelection attempts. These systematic departures from the national swing must be responsible in part for the variability noted above. But it is also apparent from Tables 5-2 and 5-3 that these incumbency effects are far from uniform. The ranges in the slump and surge figures for Democratic and Republican districts tell much of the story. Some freshmen ran well behind the national tide in 1974 while others surged ahead of it. Some incumbent successors managed to improve their party's standing while others dropped by as much as 30 percentage points. It is easy to overlook these disparities in swing figures when the focus is on seat turnover. Freshmen members were almost uniformly successful in retaining their seats in the 1976 elections, but the extent to which they improved upon their 1974 showing varied a good deal. Incumbency is a resource that pays rather uneven electoral dividends.

When these seats with pronounced incumbency effects are set aside, the total variance in swing declines but not nearly to the level recorded in the late 1950s. The standard deviation for the 1972–1974 swing in districts contested by an incumbent with at least two terms of service is 8.8 percentage points, compared to 9.6 percentage points for all districts contested both years; the standard deviation for the 1974–1976 swing is reduced from 9.0 percentage points to 6.9 percentage points when open seats and seats contested by freshmen members are eliminated. Thus the dramatic increase in the variability of partisan swing cannot be attributed wholly to the increased advantage of incumbency. The conclusion that the forces for change in district returns are to be found primarily at the local level seems unavoidable.

Table 5-3

VOTE CHANGE FOR FRESHMEN SEEKING FIRST REELECTION, 1972–1974 AND 1974–1976 ("SOPHOMORE SURGE")

(in percentage points)

Freshman's Party	1972–1974			1974–1976		
	Mean	Range	N	Mean	Range	N
Actual change						
Democrat	+13.6	+0.5 to +24.6	(10)	+4.7	−10.9 to +25.9	(70)
Republican	−0.6	−15.0 to +28.0	(36)	+10.4	−5.1 to +25.1	(17)
Adjusted for national swing[a]						
Democrat	+7.6	−5.5 to +18.6		+6.3	−9.3 to +27.5	
Republican	+5.4	−9.0 to +34.0		+8.8	−6.7 to +23.5	
All freshmen	+5.8	−9.0 to +34.0	(46)	+6.8	−9.3 to +27.5	(87)

[a] The national popular vote swing was 6.0 percentage points Democratic in 1972–1974, 1.6 percentage points Republican in 1974–1976.

Source: The definition for "sophomore surge" is taken from Cover, "Advantage," pp. 20–21. Author's calculations from official election returns.

But one question about the shape of uniform swing, a question originally raised by David Butler and Donald Stokes, remains. If voters in every district respond to a national political force in the same way, would we expect to see the same fraction of the electorate in every district shift from one party to the other? Butler and Stokes, investigating the sources of the uniform national swing in Britain, argue convincingly that, "If national influences were completely paramount, we should expect swings to involve not identical fractions of the total vote or electorate in each constituency but a fraction proportional to the prior strength of the party that was losing ground." If, for example, national forces are leading one in five Republican voters to switch to the Democratic party in 1974 while everyone else remains the same, the amount of change will be greater in districts whose electorate voted predominantly Republican in 1972 than in districts with fewer Republican voters. In Britain, where swing is nearly uniform across districts, the absence of proportional swings implies "the presence of influences which modify the effect of uniform national forces." Butler and Stokes solve this puzzle by arguing that the observed swings in Britain are "the sum, first, of the more proportional swings due to national forces, and, second, of the tendency toward homogeneity in the local constituency which retards such swings where they are strong and amplifies them where they are weak." However, the stronger the national tide, the more nearly swings are proportional to prior party strength.[3]

It is possible that some of the variance in swing in U.S. congressional elections is due not to forces whose origin is at the district level but rather to systematic national forces whose effects are mediated by the rule of proportionality to prior political strength. Table 5-4 summarizes the evidence from a crude empirical test of this proposition. Open seats and seats contested by freshmen mambers have been set aside, since we know they share unique properties related to the incumbency advantage. We want to know whether the residual variability of swing can be attributed to the proportional effects of a national political force. The 1972–1974 and 1974–1976 swings are examined within three categories of party strength defined by the results of the prior election: less than 40 percent Democratic, 40 to 60 percent Democratic, and more than 60 percent Democratic. The 1972 election is used as the base for determining prior party strength in the analysis of the 1972–1974 swing; the 1974 election is used as the base for the 1974–1976 swing. According to Butler and Stokes, the proportionality of the swing should be most apparent when the

---

[3] Butler and Stokes, *Political Change in Britain*, pp. 99–108.

Table 5-4

SWING TOWARD DEMOCRATS, BY PRIOR STRENGTH OF PARTIES, IN SEATS CONTESTED BY INCUMBENTS WITH TWO TERMS OR MORE OF SERVICE, 1972–1974, 1974–1976

(in percentage points except where stated)

Swing	Democratic Vote in Prior Elections		
	Less than 40% ("safe" Republican districts)	40% to 60% ("marginal" districts)	More than 60% ("safe" Democratic districts)
1972–1974			
Mean swing	12.6	8.0	3.8
Range	−2.0 to +36.2	−10.0 to +26.3	−16.5 to +20.2
Standard deviation	7.5	8.1	8.4
N	(78)	(58)	(74)
% of districts moving against national tide	1.3	13.8	25.7
1974–1976			
Mean swing	−2.0	−4.1	−3.9
Range	−11.7 to +15.4	−19.9 to +10.8	−25.8 to +15.1
Standard deviation	6.2	6.2	7.2
N	(47)	(72)	(104)
% of districts moving against national tide	31.9	27.8	26.0

Source: Author's calculations from official election returns.

national tide is strong, least apparent or invisible when it is weak. Consequently, we should find evidence of proportionality in the 1972–1974 swing, which registered a net popular vote shift of 6.0 percentage points to the Democrats, but not in 1974–1976 when the popular vote shift was a mere 1.6 percentage points to the Republicans.

This is precisely what we find in Table 5-4. The mean swing in 1974 increases proportionally to the prior strength of the party losing ground, namely the Republicans, while little trace of proportionality is to be found in 1976. Safe Democrats in 1974 gained on the average of 3.8 percentage points, while safe Republicans lost on the average of 12.6 percentage points. Moreover, while only one of the seventy-eight safe Republicans improved upon his 1972 margin, over a fourth of the safe Democrats actually lost ground in 1974 in spite of the strong national tide favoring their party. This helps explain why the vanishing marginals phenomenon of recent years did not significantly distort the vote/seat ratio in the 1974 election. A fundamental property of strong national tides is to amplify swings in districts dominated by the party losing ground, so a national swing of 6.0 percentage points can leave its mark well outside the marginal range as it is traditionally defined. These findings help explain why presumably safe incumbents of both parties feel such great uncertainty about their electoral prospects in any given year. Individual incumbents of the party losing ground nationally realize that their own vote losses can easily run much higher than the national swing; individual incumbents of the party gaining ground know that they are unlikely to reap the full rewards of the national tide and that they may actually lose ground.

Although in 1974 district swings on the average were proportional to prior political strength, there was ample room for district variation. For example, two adjoining districts in Kentucky, both represented by Republican incumbents who had captured 74 percent of the vote in 1972, had widely divergent swings as a result of the 1974 election: one incumbent lost four percentage points while the other ran twenty-two percentage points behind his 1972 vote. The source of this difference can be found only at the district level, in the reputation of the candidates and the effectiveness of their campaigns. Even when national tides are strong, local forces can obliterate their effect.

On the basis of this examination of the 1974 and 1976 congressional elections, there is ample justification for focusing on district-level determinants of electoral change. Analyses of congressional election outcomes that deal only with changes in the national division of the two-party vote, such as the work of Edward Tufte,[4] omit by definition factors that are of enormous political importance to incumbents and challengers alike. It is to these factors that we now turn.

Candidates and Election Outcomes in Sample Districts

A clear inference from the analysis of individual vote choice in the last chapter is that the primary district-level determinant of electoral change is the relative attractiveness of the candidates. However, the evidence upon which this conclusion is based is limited in several respects: survey data from only ten congressional districts were used in the analysis and no attempt was made to link shifts in public attitudes toward the candidates with changes in the actual vote in

---

[4] Tufte, *Political Control of the Economy.*

these congressional districts. If the appropriate data—district-level indicators of candidate reputation and party identification for pairs of elections in a probability sample of congressional districts—were available, it would be possible to trace directly the impact of public attitudes on electoral change. However, the cost of sampling opinion in a large number of congressional districts is so high that it is unlikely such data will ever be available. We must resign ourselves to making reasonable inferences based on the information at hand.

Up to this point I have demonstrated that large numbers of voters have positive or negative impressions of congressional candidates and that these impressions are directly related to vote choice. The former inference is based on surveys in approximately forty districts, the latter on surveys in ten districts. I have also shown that congressional district election returns between 1972 and 1976 reveal that the forces behind a lion's share of the electoral change that occurred originated at the district level; this conclusion, of course, is based on all districts contested by both the major parties in succeeding elections. What remains to be done is to investigate whether the electoral outcomes in districts for which I have some survey data reflect the relative public standing of the candidates. The small number of cases and the absence of measures at more than one election and of data on some important indicators preclude a robust multivariate analysis of the determinants of electoral change in these districts. Instead, my strategy will be to examine those districts whose election returns diverge sharply from the partisan balance in the district for evidence of the impact of candidate actions and public reactions.

How Closely Do Electoral Returns Mirror the Distribution of Partisans?

Party identification is a useful baseline from which to assess the impact of public attitudes towards the candidates at the district as well as the individual level. The distribution of partisans within congressional districts is generally thought to be the major determinant of which party wins and by what margin. However, since direct measures of the number of Democratic and Republican identifiers within congressional districts have seldom been taken, this generalization must be inferred from an analysis of individual identification and behavior in samples of the national congressional electorate. The availability of surveys in forty-two congressional districts provides a unique opportunity to see whether the party with the most identifiers always controls the congressional seat.

In the analysis that follows, as in earlier chapters, I have treated Independent leaners as partisans; pure Independents are excluded from the computation of the partisan advantage, which is defined simply as the difference in the percentages of the electorate identifying with the two parties. Although these districts cluster in the competitive range in terms of actual votes, a partisan advantage of greater than ten percentage points is present in a majority of them. (The actual frequencies are as follows: 0–5 percentage point advantage, 11 districts; 6–10 percentage point advantage, 9 districts; 11+ percentage point advantage, 22 districts.) In about a third of these districts (15 in 1974, 13 in 1976) the minority party—that with fewer partisan identifiers—won the election. In 1974, the year of the strong Democratic tide, eight of these fifteen seats were won by Republicans. This alone is impressive evidence of the influence of individual candidacies. However, the magnitude of the departure of the vote from the partisan balance of the district must also be considered.

Since we expect incumbents to run better than the partisan base in their districts, they ought to be examined separately from open seat contestants. Let P_I be the percentage of the electorate identifying with the party of the incumbent; P_C the percentage identifying with the party of the challenger; V_I the percentage of the vote cast for the incumbent; and V_C the percentage of the vote cast for the challenger. $P_I - P_C$ then is the incumbent's partisan advantage (or disadvantage); $(V_I - V_C) - (P_I - P_C)$ measures the extent to which an incumbent runs better (or worse) than the balance of party identifiers in his district. If we define an incumbent's expected base vote as his party identifiers (P_I) plus one-half of the pure Independents, it is easy to demonstrate that $[(V_I - V_C) - (P_I - P_C)]/2$ equals the difference between the incumbent's actual vote and his expected base vote.[5]

---

[5] Let A_I be the incumbent advantage and $E(V_I)$ the incumbent's expected base vote.

$$A_I = V_I - E(V_I)$$
$$= V_I - \left(P_I + \frac{\text{Independents}}{2}\right)$$
$$= V_I - \left(P_I + \frac{100 - P_I - P_C}{2}\right)$$
$$= \frac{2V_I - 100 - P_I + P_C}{2}$$
$$= \frac{V_I - (100 - V_I) - (P_I - P_C)}{2}$$
$$= \frac{(V_I - V_C) - (P_I - P_C)}{2}$$

The figures in Table 5-5 demonstrate that incumbents usually attract a higher percentage of the vote than the political complexion of their districts merits, but as many as a third run below this partisan advantage. The magnitude of the mean incumbency advantage—five percentage points in 1974 and six percentage points in 1976—is in line with estimates made by Erikson from an entirely different set of calculations,[6] but once again this measure of central tendency hides as much as it reveals. The range in the difference between actual vote and expected vote is more than fifty percentage points in both 1974 and 1976. Some incumbents have made safe seats of what by the balance of partisan identifiers ought to be competitive or opposition party seats. Others have allowed relatively safe seats to slip into the competitive range.

The few open seat contests that fall in this sample of districts (ten in 1974, six in 1976) complicate any comparison with seats contested by an incumbent. Nonetheless, several findings are worth noting. In one-fourth of these open seat contests (four out of sixteen) the minority party candidate won the election. The departure of the vote from the underlying partisan balance in each district was considerably smaller than in seats with incumbents running; the mean of the absolute difference between vote advantage and partisan advantage was ten percentage points in open seats, twenty percentage points in incumbent-contested seats. Yet in several cases the difference between the balance of partisans and the vote was as large as the upper limit witnessed for incumbents. In general, the outcomes of open seat races more nearly reflect the partisan cast of the districts than do the results of incumbent races, but the potential for substantial influence by open seat candidates is present.

When we examine the extreme cases—those in which the vote departs most dramatically from the underlying partisan distribution—several patterns emerge. In a number of Southern and border districts, Republican candidates facing electorates with anywhere from two and one-half to four times as many Democrats as Republicans still attract a large percentage of the votes. Some Republican incumbents have fashioned safe seats out of these natural Democratic strongholds; other Republican challengers have pulled Democratic incumbents well into the competitive range. In all of these districts the Republican base extends well beyond the small portion of the electorate that identifies with the Republican party.

---

[6] This provides a striking external validity check on my own limited data set. Erikson, "Advantage of Incumbency in Congressional Elections," pp. 623–632.

Table 5-5

RELATIONSHIP BETWEEN VOTE AND PARTISAN BALANCE
IN SEATS CONTESTED BY INCUMBENTS, 1974 AND 1976

("advantage" figures in percentage points)

	1974	1976	Formula[a]
No. of incumbents who ran *above* partisan advantage	21	23	$(V_I - V_C) > (P_I - P_C)$
No. of incumbents who ran *below* partisan advantage	10	13	$(V_I - V_C) < (P_I - P_C)$
Advantage of incumbency Mean	5	6	$\dfrac{(V_I - V_C) - (P_I - P_C)}{2}$
Range	−14 to +39	−20 to +32	

[a] V_I is the incumbent's percentage of the vote; V_C is the challenger's percentage of the vote; P_I is the percentage of the electorate identifying with the incumbent's party; and P_C is the percentage of the electorate identifying with the challenger's party.

Source: DSG surveys and official election returns.

In other districts the discrepancy between the vote and partisan balance reflects the ability of some incumbents to cut deeply into the partisan base of their opponents. But if some incumbents succeed in this fashion, why not all? The answer must turn on the visibility and appeal within the electorate of the incumbent and challenger, a matter explored in greater detail below.

A final pattern occurs in open seat contests, in which candidates of the dominant party in the district run either well ahead of or well behind their natural party base. In one district a new candidate attracted a larger percentage of the vote than the safe incumbent whom he had succeeded as the party's nominee. In another district when the incumbent retired, his successor, after beginning the campaign with a considerable edge in visibility, ran well under the partisan base and far behind the incumbent's percentage in previous elections. In both cases the campaigns were decisive in leading to outcomes substantially at odds with the division of partisans in the electorate.

The departure of the vote from the partisan division in each district should be partly related to aggregate measures of candidate visibility and attractiveness. The existence of this relationship at the individual level was demonstrated in Chapter 4. Here I am looking at a larger number of districts with a different unit of analysis to see if the same association is present. Most of the findings are based on 1976 data, although contrasting information from 1974 is used when appropriate.

Table 5-6 presents the mean incumbency advantage, defined as the difference between the incumbent's actual vote and his expected base with different levels of candidate name recall.[7] Incumbents generally run well ahead of their partisan base when they are salient to the voters in their districts and when their challengers are not. The electoral benefit is especially pronounced when both conditions are present—the eight incumbents who enjoyed a name-recall advantage of more than thirty percentage points over their opponents ran on the average of thirteen percentage points better than their partisan base.[8] As we would expect from the results of the analysis of individual vote choice in Chapter 4, the relationship between candidate visibility and the vote is far from perfect. Some highly visible incumbents and challengers evoke a sharply negative response from the public and consequently fail to reap any electoral harvest from their saliency. But the evidence does support the proposition that the victory margins of many incumbents are inflated by the low visibility of their challengers.

Measures of candidate reputation are even more accurate predictors of the incumbent's success in running ahead of his partisan base.[9] In 1976 the eleven incumbents who achieved favorable job ratings higher than 55 percent won on the average eight percentage points more of the vote than predicted by the partisan division in their districts. The advantage of incumbency vanishes beneath this job approval level. A similar cutoff point is present on the incumbent feeling thermometer (see Table 5-7). Those incumbents who failed to hold a lead over their challengers of at least twenty percentage points in the percentage of positive ratings obtained no more votes than the partisan division in their districts would otherwise dictate.

---

[7] In Tables 5-6 and 5-7, the categories are constructed in order both to preserve significant differences in the dependent variable and to distribute districts evenly into the several categories. When these goals collide, the former takes precedence.
[8] Part of the reason the difference in candidate name recall is more strongly related to the incumbent's electoral advantage than the incumbent's name recall alone is that the former measure is not affected by saliency fluctuations due to variations in district media structure.
[9] Incumbent job rating and incumbent positive thermometer are both more strongly related to the incumbent's electoral advantage (that is, his success in running ahead of his partisan base) than incumbent name recall. However, the relationship between the difference in candidate reputation and the incumbent's electoral advantage is weaker than for the difference in candidate name recall. This occurs for two reasons: the absence of significant variation in the challenger positive thermometer and the underlying association between party identification and candidate reputation.

Table 5-6

MEAN INCUMBENT ADVANTAGE, BY CANDIDATE VISIBILITY, IN SELECTED DISTRICTS, 1976

(in percentage points)

Candidate's Visibility	Mean Incumbent Advantage[a]	N
Incumbent name recall		
55% or more	7	(10)
45% to 54%	6	(7)
less than 45%	2	(12)
Challenger name recall		
40% or more	−1	(5)
20% to 39%	8	(7)
less than 20%	7	(13)
Incumbent name recall minus challenger name recall		
more than 30 percentage points	13	(8)
20 to 30 percentage points	2	(10)
less than 20 percentage points	1	(6)

[a] Incumbent advantage is defined as the difference between the incumbent's actual vote and his partisan base, that is, $\dfrac{(V_I - V_C) - (P_I - P_C)}{2}$, where V_I is the incumbent's percentage of the vote; V_C is the challenger's percentage of the vote; P_I is the percentage of the electorate identifying with the incumbent's party; and P_C is the percentage of the electorate identifying with the challenger's party.
Source: DSG surveys.

In most of these 1976 contests, the incumbents held substantial advantages in both visibility and reputation; only eight of the twenty-eight challengers evoked positive feelings from more than 20 percent of the electorate while only one of the incumbents fell beneath this level of support. One should not conclude, however, that this is the inevitable fate of challengers. There were important exceptions among these 1976 challengers. And the six challengers whose districts I surveyed in 1974 achieved very high levels of recognition and support. The fact that the incumbents in these six districts ran on the average of three percentage points behind their partisan base can undoubtedly be attributed to national as well as district forces. But it is important to note that all six challengers were widely recognized and highly regarded in their districts well before the election. Incumbents have at their disposal resources that can be used to produce impressive advan-

Table 5-7
MEAN INCUMBENT ADVANTAGE, BY CANDIDATE REPUTATION, SELECTED DISTRICTS, 1976
(in percentage points)

Candidate's Reputation	Mean Incumbent Advantage[a]	N
Incumbent Favorable Job Rating		
more than 55%	8	(11)
45% to 55%	1	(10)
less than 45%	−1	(6)
Incumbent Positive Thermometer		
50% or more	8	(13)
40% to 49%	1	(7)
less than 40%	1	(8)
Challenger Positive Thermometer		
more than 30%	−3	(3)
20% to 30%	9	(5)
less than 20%	5	(20)
Incumbent Positive Thermometer Minus		
Challenger Positive Thermometer		
more than 30%	8	(8)
20% to 30%	8	(8)
less than 20%	0	(9)

[a] Incumbent advantage is defined as the difference between the incumbent's actual vote and his partisan base, that is, $\dfrac{(V_I - V_C) - (P_I - P_C)}{2}$, where V_I is the incumbent's percentage of the vote; V_C is the challenger's percentage of the vote; P_I is the percentage of the electorate identifying with the incumbent's party; and P_C is the percentage of the electorate identifying with the challenger's party.
Source: DSG surveys.

tages, but these advantages can be neutralized either by the incumbents' mistakes or by effective opposition.

This concludes my investigation of how much congressional election outcomes depart from the underlying partisan division in each district and why. There is considerable evidence to support the view that public responses to congressional candidates lead to district votes substantially at odds with the underlying division of partisans. And from this we can reasonably infer that the same forces are largely responsible for the nonuniform interelection district swings discussed in the first part of this chapter. Since I do not have survey measures of candidate visibility and reputation in the same districts for two consecutive elections, I am unable to determine directly the sources of this swing. But the evidence at hand is quite persuasive that much of the electoral change that occurs in congressional districts is a result of the voters' reactions to the candidates in their districts.[10]

---

[10] While to some this conclusion might appear to belabor the obvious, it is offered here as a corrective to a large body of literature arguing that party and incumbency "explain" congressional elections. When candidate saliency (narrowly defined) failed to account for the increased electoral value of incumbency, scholars turned away from public attitudes toward the candidates as a determinant of voting in congressional elections. The findings discovered here at both the individual and the district level argue strongly for a resurrection of the candidate in congressional election research.

6
Conclusions

Summary

Virtually all studies of congressional elections heretofore have concentrated on the behavior of individual voters in a national sample or on aggregate change in the national vote for Congress. This study, adopting the perspective of the candidates themselves, focuses instead on the district. From this angle, it soon becomes obvious that party and national tides are woefully inadequate for explaining the voters' choices in congressional elections.

The first task was to discover what the public knows about the candidates. The conventional wisdom is that it knows very little. My investigation of the electorates in some forty districts, however, led me to conclude that the public is more aware of congressional candidates than we have believed. Large numbers of voters have impressions of the candidates, however partial the information at hand. These perceptions reflect the political dialogue in the constituency, which is itself generated in part by the candidates.

But do people's impressions of the candidates determine how they vote? What about party loyalty, incumbency, and simple name identification—usually said to account for virtually all voting in congressional elections? My analysis of data on all of these factors in ten congressional districts confirmed that it is candidate preference that most consistently correlates with vote choice. Party alone accounts for relatively few votes—and party defection and Independent voting in line with candidate preference are on the rise. Even when candidate preference and party coincide, as they so often do, the manner in which our data were gathered permits us to infer that candidate preference is not an automatic expression of party loyalty. Apparently many more voters than we had realized make judgments about the candidates unrelated to party.

Turning to changes in election outcomes, I soon discovered that the pattern of change in all contested districts is highly irregular. The national swing is a relatively poor predictor of swing in individual districts. Clearly we are witnessing an increasing localization of political forces in congressional elections. Even in 1974, when the national tide was running strong for the Democrats, Republican candidates improved on their party's margin in one-fifth of the districts. What is more, the amount of variation in swing across districts has tripled in the last two decades. Moving back to the districts in which DSG surveys had been conducted, I was able to identify as the source of much of this local variation in swing the public's assessments of the candidates. Increasingly, then, congressmen are responsible for their own margins of victory or defeat, and the electoral constraints they face are defined in their own districts.

Implications

It is a fundamental tenet of our democratic system that governmental leaders are held accountable to the citizens they represent through the electoral process. This process of forcing incumbent leaders to publicly compete for the legitimate right to hold office provides the most effective guarantee that the leaders' actions will correspond in some way to the preferences of the citizens. What happens to that accountability, however, when this potential sanction loses its teeth? This is the question raised at least implicitly by the recent commentary on the decline of competitive elections and the increase in the advantage of incumbency. Of course, incumbent House members have been enormously successful at the polls for many years. But recent shifts in the structure of competition have led many observers to believe that the credibility of an opposition threat may have been even further weakened. If incumbents have lost all sense of electoral insecurity, hasn't the basis of accountability been seriously eroded?

This argument rests upon the assumption that electoral insecurity is an objective fact, or at least a state of mind that can be predicted accurately from objective measures. By this standard, for example, a congressman who wins reelection with say 60 or 65 percent of the vote is "safe" and ought to be relatively unconcerned about the threat of the next challenger. Yet we know that politicians overwhelmingly reject this assumption. John Kingdon and Richard Fenno have both observed the tremendous uncertainty congressmen feel about reelection, regardless of their electoral margins.[1] And David Mayhew has argued that "it is possible to conceive of an assembly in which no

[1] Kingdon, *Congressmen's Voting Decisions*, pp. 59–64; Fenno, *Home Style*.

member ever comes close to losing a seat but in which the need to be reelected is what inspires members' behavior. It would be an assembly with no saints or fools in it, an assembly packed with skilled politicians going about their business."[2] These authors have suggested various reasons why congressmen remain insecure even in what appear to be safe seats; they have also described how congressmen act to insure their continued electoral support. These persuasive arguments for the validity of subjective measures of marginality have been based almost entirely on politicians' beliefs about voters.

The research reported in this book provides evidence in support of the same arguments, based upon the voters' views of the politicians. It is much easier to understand congressmen's constant concern about reelection once we reject the notion of massive public ignorance among the congressional electorate. If voters choose the preferred candidate in congressional elections instead of automatically voting their party or bowing to the incumbent, then congressmen have little basis for judging themselves invulnerable. Candidate saliency is a double-edged sword for incumbents; while it can mean an enormous advantage in visibility over challengers, it can also spell disaster if the voters come to believe that their representative has some personal failing. We have seen that the latter is not just a theoretical possibility. By several standards other than reelection itself—margin of victory, job ratings, public image, and so on—the record of incumbents is very uneven. Some actually run well below the natural partisan base in their districts, and none can count on incumbency alone to see him through a serious challenge. Voters are sufficiently discriminating to make congressmen wary of the possible public reaction to their actions in office.

Does this mean, then, that we should be reassured about the nature of voting in congressional elections, that all is well because voters are sufficiently attentive and incumbents are sufficiently wary? The answer to this question surely is no. There is reason to worry about the quality of the deliberation behind the public's choice of candidates, the diminishing electoral connection between congressmen and their party and President, and the implications of both for the ability of Congress to do its legislative work.

We have seen that most voters acquire enough information to evaluate the congressional candidates in their district, although these evaluations are usually barren of policy content. Critics of Congress have long believed that this is the way incumbents want it to be: House members use the resources of their office to advertise themselves and take credit for delivering federal largesse to their districts or for

---

[2] Mayhew, *Congress*, p. 37.

helping individual constituents with problems, all the while glossing over areas of conflict. In recent years, it is said, the public-relations orientation of newer members has fostered a heavy reliance on the media, on direct mail, and on growing personal staffs to convey favorable images to the electorate. All of these activities tend to reward the incumbent without doing much to improve the quality of the public's thinking about the candidates.

The research reported in this book cautions against looking exclusively at the incumbent's activities in office. Public opinion can change in response to actions taken by either incumbent or challenger or to external events during the campaign itself. Yet while such actions and events may change public attitudes, they will not necessarily enlighten the electorate. In their search for publicity, the life blood of their campaigns, candidates often resort to gimmicks of one kind or another—walking, work days, posturing in front of symbolic places—that might catch the attention of the local television news crew. The availability of detailed information on campaign contributions and expenditures, meanwhile, offers candidates virtually unlimited opportunities for making sensational charges about their opponents' ethical propriety. As congressional campaigns become more and more divorced from local party organizations and more and more dependent upon the mass media, the likelihood increases that voters' decisions will turn on personal qualities of the candidates (real or alleged) that are not central to the job of the representative.

The style of modern campaigning is also unlikely to do much to enhance the electorate's view of political institutions. In an era of mass cynicism toward authority and institutions, candidates are increasingly taking pains to separate themselves from their party, their President, and the Congress itself. Richard Fenno has noted that congressmen run for reelection by running against the Congress. More generally, candidates play on public cynicism by identifying themselves as opponents of the institutions to which they aspire to belong. They enhance their own images, and hence gain electoral strength, by attacking the authorities and institutions with responsibility for governing. It works, at least in the short run. The public's approval ratings of Congress are low, while its ratings of most individual congressmen are high. But it seems likely that one can run down the institution of which one is a part only so long before becoming a victim of one's own rhetoric.

One cause and effect of these changes in the nature of campaigning is the weakening of the discipline formerly provided by the ties between congressional candidates, on the one hand, and political parties and presidential candidates on the other. Both the longstanding ties

104

and their recent decomposition are well documented. The proportion of districts carried by a presidential nominee of one party and a House nominee of another increased from 14.1 percent in 1932 to 28.5 percent in 1976, hitting a peak of 44.1 percent in 1972.[3] Between a quarter and a third of all votes cast for the House are other than party-line votes, and a significant number of seats are won by candidates of the minority party in the district.

The costs of this decomposition go beyond depriving the voter of a simple way of making rational choices between candidates. Its effects are felt as well in the failure of elections to authorize governments to govern. The debate over the nature of representation, of course, is an old one. Is the purpose of elections to allow disparate communities to choose spokesmen for their interests or to allow a nation to empower a government (in a country like Britain, a political party) to rule? While members of the House have traditionally represented the people in both of these ways, the clear implication of recent electoral history and the research reported in this book is that the former has become dominant and the latter increasingly weak.[4]

Certainly this is the case in the present Congress. Members have highly individualistic instincts, born of their own electoral experiences and fueled by the dispersion of power and the increase of staff resources in recent years. Reforms strengthening the formal powers of the party leadership in the House have failed to stem this growing individualism, and the President has been conspicuously unsuccessful in leading a party government that reaches across the two branches. Meanwhile, Congress is doing as well as ever at representing discrete district interests; in this sense, recent developments may have actually "strengthened a congressional strength."[5] The charge that as a result of the advantages of incumbency the Congress has become insulated from and unresponsive to public opinion is wide of the mark. On the contrary, the members are now more than ever likely to represent their constituents' interests at all stages of the legislative process.

Allen Schick has observed that although Congress is doing more, it is accomplishing less.[6] The number of roll call votes is higher than ever, but the number of new public laws is down. More important, Con-

---

[3] Mayhew, "Congressional Representation," p. 268, and *Congressional Quarterly Weekly Report*, April 22, 1978, p. 972.

[4] David Mayhew made this point some years ago in "Congressional Representation" in which he distinguished "representation by reflection" from "representation by authorization."

[5] Richard F. Fenno, Jr., "Strengthening a Congressional Strength," in *Congress Reconsidered*, Dodd and Oppenheimer, eds., pp. 261–268.

[6] Allen Schick, in a talk to the American Political Science Association Congressional Fellows, 1978.

gress has disposed of few of the major legislative initiatives of the new Democratic administration. Many factors contribute to this legislative stalemate, including the lack of public consensus and the personal failings of the President. But one critically important element is the breakdown in the electoral connection between congressmen and their party and President. The mandate defined by congressional elections calls for representing and protecting individuals and groups, not for joining with the President to develop national policy. Consequently, the movement on Capitol Hill is towards restricting the President—with congressional vetoes, sunset laws, annual authorizations, and riders on appropriations bills—rather than towards cooperating with him. The separation of powers is exacerbated in the absence of the unifying influence of party government.

The Future

What are the prospects for significant changes in congressional elections? Will competition for seats in the House of Representatives increase? If so, how will this affect Congress's capacity to govern?

In light of the present advantages of incumbency and of the resourcefulness of officeholders in preserving the resources they now have, most observers doubt that House elections will become more competitive in the foreseeable future. To be sure, there will be turnover, but most of this will come from retirements, as more and more members find the pace and the lifestyle not to their liking.

My own view is different. I believe House elections may very well become more like Senate elections, where the advantages of incumbency are often neutralized by highly visible, well-financed challengers and where turnover due to electoral defeat is far from insignificant. Several important prerequisites of increased competition in House elections are already present, notably a decline in the importance of party identification and an increase in the candidate orientation of voters. Right now, both factors disproportionately favor incumbents, but this need not always be so. One need look only at the experience of most Presidents and some senators to sense the possibility of diminishing returns from constant publicity. There is direct evidence of this in the House itself: the electoral fate of Richard Nixon's defenders on the House Judiciary Committee makes one wonder about the ultimate effects of televising the proceedings of the House.

Yet an increase in competition depends most upon the efforts of the challengers. At the present time, many House seats are not seriously contested. A review of campaign expenditure figures confirms this fact. Challengers in the November 1976 House elections spent an average of $49,000, compared with $80,000 for incumbents; over 40 percent of these challengers spent less than $20,000. The lack of competition in many districts reflects the decision by local elites not to mount a serious challenge.

When challengers do make the effort and spend money, it makes a difference. Gary Jacobson has demonstrated that in House elections

> spending by challengers has a substantial impact on election outcomes, whereas spending by incumbents has relatively little effect. . . . The more incumbents spend, the worse they do; the reason is that they raise and spend money in direct proportion to the magnitude of the electoral threat posed by the challenger, but this reactive spending fails to offset the progress made by the challenger that inspires it in the first place.[7]

It is not important whether the incumbent spends more than the challenger; what matters is the actual level of spending by the challenger. The implications for public policy, as noted by Jacobson, are clear: in order to increase competition, we must increase the challengers' funds, either with public subsidies or with measures that make it easier for challengers to raise money. Limiting contributions and putting ceilings on spending will only dampen competition further.

If public financing of congressional elections without overly restrictive ceilings on expenditures comes to pass in the next several years, the level of competition should increase significantly. Even if the proposal for public subsidies fails, it should be only a matter of time before those out of power in congressional districts find the resources to offer more vigorous opposition. And since voters are increasingly disposed to cast their ballots on the basis of candidate evaluation, highly visible, well-financed challengers should be able to alter the structure of competition now with us.

If I am correct and competition in House elections does increase, will our democratic processes be enhanced? I think not. Increased competition based not on the reputation of the parties but on the relative attractiveness of the local candidates will do nothing to alter the individualistic tone of the present-day Congress. Congressmen may have to work harder than ever to please the voters in their districts, but this will not necessarily strengthen the capacity of our political institutions to govern.

---

[7] Gary C. Jacobson, "The Effects of Campaign Spending in Congressional Elections," *American Political Science Review*, vol. 72 (June 1978), p. 469.

APPENDIX

The Democratic Study Group Congressional District Surveys

The survey data used in this study were gathered for congressional candidates by the Democratic Study Group Campaign Fund. All of the surveys were directed either by myself or by David Cooper; the entire polling program was under the supervision of DSG Executive Director Richard Conlon. All of the surveys conducted in 1974 and 1976 are listed in this appendix.

With the single exception of sampling, which is discussed in detail below, all of the procedures used in the surveys followed normal professional practice. The interviews were conducted from central telephone banks by trained volunteers between the hours of 6:00 p.m. and 9:30 p.m. In almost all cases they were completed in less than a week. Supervisors were present to check the quality of interviewing and to edit the completed questionnaires. Since all items were pre-coded, keypunching was done directly from the edited questionnaires.

In 1976 each survey was designed to obtain completed interviews with a sample of 400 likely voters; in 1974 the sample size was 300. Respondents were chosen in three stages: selection of households, selection of respondents within households, and determination of whether respondents were likely to vote in the November election. When an official list of registered voters served as the sampling frame, the first two stages were combined. For a majority of the surveys, district telephone directories served as the sampling frame, and it was necessary to devise a procedure for determining who within the household was to be interviewed. In both cases, the need to complete all interviews within several days necessitated choosing replacements for those respondents who, for one reason or another, could not be interviewed during this time. Actually, a large number of calls failed to produce a completed interview, usually because the potential respondent was not at home, but sometimes because he was found to be in-

CONGRESSIONAL DISTRICTS SURVEYED BY THE DEMOCRATIC STUDY GROUP, 1974–1976

Congressional District	No. of Surveys	Date of Surveys	Preelection Incumbency Status		Election Winner	Form of Data	
			Party	No. of terms		Summary figures	Raw data
1974							
Ala. 1	1	Oct.	R	5	R	X	
Ind. 8	1	Aug.	R	4	D	X	
Iowa 2	1	July	Open Seat		D	X	
Iowa 3	1	July	Open Seat		R	X	
Iowa 5	2	June, Oct.	R	4	D	X	
Iowa 6	1	June	R	4	D	X	
Md. 5	1	Aug.	Open Seat		D	X	
Mich. 12	2	Jan., Sept.	D	8	D	X	
N.J. 1	2	July, Oct.	R	4	D	X	
N.J. 2	2	July, Oct.	R	4	D	X	
Ohio 8	1	Oct.	Open Seat		R	X	
Va. 10	1	Sept.	R	11	R	X	
Wash. 6	1	Aug.	D	5	D	X	
1976							
Ala. 2	1	Oct.	R	6	R	X	
Calif. 16	3	Apr., July, Oct.	R	7	D	X	
Calif. 35	3	Jan., May, Sept.	D	1	D	X	
Conn. 2	1	June	D	1	D	X	
Ill. 3	3	May, Aug., Oct.	D	1	D	X	
Ill. 10	4	Nov. (1975), Apr., Aug., Sept.	D	1	D	X	

State			Elections					
Ill.	15	1	May	D	1	R		X
Ind.	6	4	Nov. (1975), May, Aug., Sept.	D	1	D	X	X
Ind.	8	1	Sept.	Open Seat		D		
Iowa	5	2	May, Sept.	D	1	D	X	
Kans.	2	3	Nov. (1975), Apr., Sept.	D	1	D		X
Kans.	4	3	Aug., Sept., Oct.	R	8	R	X	X
Maine	1	2	July, Sept.	R	1	R	X	
Md.	1	1	Sept.	R	1½	R		X
Md.	5	4	Nov. (1975), Mar, Sept., Oct.	D	1	D	X	X
Minn.	6	3	Mar., Aug., Oct.	D	1	D	X	
Mont.	1	2	Nov. (1975), Aug.	D	1	D	X	X
Mont.	2	1	Aug.	Open Seat		R	X	
Neb.	2	3	June, Sept., Oct.	Open Seat		D	X	X
N.J.	2	2	May, Sept.	D	1	D	X	X
N.J.	13	3	Mar., Sept., Oct.	D	1	D	X	
N.Y.	3	2	July, Oct.	D	1	D	X	
N.Y.	5	1	July	R	7	R	X	
N.Y.	27	4	Nov. (1975), Apr., July, Sept.	D	1	D	X	X
N.Y.	29	4	Nov. (1975), May, Aug., Sept.	D	1	D	X	X
N.Y.	39	2	June, Oct.	D	½	D	X	
N.C.	5	4	Nov. (1975), May, Sept., Oct.	D	1	D	X	X
Ohio	9	2	Aug., Oct.	D	11	D		X

Congressional District	No. of Surveys	Date of Surveys	Preelection Incumbency Status Party	Preelection Incumbency Status No. of terms	Election Winner	Form of Data Summary figures	Form of Data Raw data
(1976 con't)							
Pa. 18	2	July, Oct.	Open Seat		D		X
Tenn. 3	2	Mar., Sept.	D	1	D		X
Tex. 8	1	July	D	5	D	X	
Utah 2	2	Nov. (1975), Aug.	D	1	R	X	
Va. 8	3	Mar., Aug., Sept.	D	1	D	X	
Va. 10	2	May, Sept.	D	1	D		X

Summary	*1974*	*1976*
No. of districts	13	34
No. of surveys	17	81
No. with raw data available		
Districts	0	13
Surveys	0	29

eligible (not likely to vote in the election) or because he refused to be interviewed. The total number of unsuccessful calls varied substantially across districts but averaged twice the sample size, or about 800 in 1976. Between 10 and 20 percent were due to outright refusals.

As often as possible, each district was "stratified," that is, divided into parts that were internally homogeneous in a political sense and externally heterogeneous. The number of interviews completed in each stratum was proportional to its likely contribution to the district's total vote. This contribution was determined from turnout in the election four years prior to the upcoming election, unless substantial population changes required a more current measure. I should note that in some districts lists of registered voters were unavailable and it was impossible to stratify because all households were included in a single telephone directory. In these few cases, we took special care to check the representativeness of the sample after the interviews were completed.

When the sampling frame was the list of all registered voters, the procedure was relatively straightforward. Since in all cases these names were stored on computers, instructions were given to print every nth name within each stratum, n being the number of names on that part of the list divided by three times the number of completed interviews required. Telephone numbers were then obtained from telephone directories or the information operator. Interviews were taken only with the person selected from the list of registered voters, not with any other person in the household. Before the interview was conducted, these respondents had to pass through a likely-voter screen: only registered voters who had turned out in the previous election and who intended to do so in the upcoming election were selected. Calls were made in each stratum until the desired number of completed interviews was obtained.

When the sampling frame was the set of all congressional district telephone numbers listed in published directories, the procedure was more complex. The same stratification strategy was used, but in this case each stratum was assigned the appropriate number of "sample points." The sample point was a page from a telephone directory from which six interviews were to be obtained. The numbers were selected at random from each page. Interviewers were faced with the task of determining who within the household associated with the telephone number selected in the sample should be designated as respondent. A quota for sex was used; for each sample point, interviews were obtained with three men and three women. Furthermore, the pool of eligible respondents within each household was defined as all persons eighteen years or older living in the household and at home when the interviewer called. Since in about 80 percent of all households only one person of a particular sex met this requirement, and since the probability of younger persons' being out between the hours of 6:00 p.m. and 9:30 p.m. was high, an arbitrary but empirically reliable selection procedure was devised. Interviewers were instructed to select the youngest eligible person of the same sex as the person answering the telephone, unless the quota for that sex had already been filled. If it had, the youngest eligible person of the other sex was selected. The effect of this procedure was that the person answering the phone was interviewed in about 80 percent of the cases and a younger adult in the remaining cases, except when a particular sex quota was filled.

All of these procedures—replacement, sex quotas, selection of youngest adult present at the time of the call—removed the sample from a strict probability basis; therefore the sampling error could not be estimated the usual way. The best test of the reliability of our sample was to gauge its representativeness along certain demographic and political dimensions. By these standards, the surveys stood up quite well. It was particularly reassuring to find little change in the marginal distribution of party identification, age, race, and income in successive surveys of the same district. Moreover, the pattern of responses across many congressional districts was coherent.

Since the DSG congressional district polls were conducted for candidates on a strictly confidential basis, the data upon which this book is based cannot be made available to the scholarly community. I regret this limitation, and I hope that soon we will not have to rely on private polls for the study of public opinion in congressional elections.

INDEX

Localization of political forces. *See* National swing

Marginal districts: study findings not limited to, 5–6. *See also* Districts, competitiveness of; "Vanishing marginals"
Mayhew, David, 6n, 16, 17, 18n, 21, 71, 72, 82, 85, 87, 102, 103, 105n
McGovern, George, 22
Media market, 28–29, 33, 46, 96
Midterm elections: loss of seats by President's party, 1; as referendums on performance of President, 1–2, 4, 12–14. *See also* Economy; Presidential popularity; "Surge and decline"
Miller, Arthur, 13
Miller, Warren E., 1n, 11, 12, 13, 15, 16, 23, 26, 34, 38, 44, 55, 56, 74n

Name recognition. *See* Candidate saliency
National swing: in Britain and United States, 85; proportional to prior party strength, 89–91; uniformity of, 2, 7, 19, 82–88
Nelson, Candice J., 16, 17
Nixon, Richard, 22, 37, 46, 73, 106

Open seats, 21, 28, 33, 43, 51, 85–87, 93–95
Oppenheimer, Bruce I., 18n
Ornstein, Norman, 41n

Page, Benjamin, 44
Party decomposition, 104–105
Party defection, 12–14, 20–21, 49, 53–62; incumbent advantage in, 13, 54

Party identification, 4, 12–14, 19–20, 36, 49–50, 65, 67, 69–70; distribution within congressional districts, 92–99
Party-line voting, 12–14, 49–50. *See also* Party defection; Party identification
Polsby, Nelson W., 17n
Presidential coattails, 19–20, 70; separation of presidential and congressional vote, 3, 104–105
Presidential popularity, 1–2, 4

Redistricting, 17
Retirements, 82, 106; increase in since 1972, 3
"Retirement slump," 85–87

Schick, Allen, 105
Schoenberger, Robert A., 22
Seniority, 29–30
"Sophomore surge," 18, 87–88
Stokes, Donald, 1n, 11, 12, 13, 15, 16, 19, 20n, 22n, 23, 26, 34, 38, 44n, 55, 56, 74n, 85, 89
"Surge and decline," 1, 2, 12
Surveys: procedures, 109–111; sponsorship of, 5–6; timing of, 50

Tufte, Edward, 1, 2, 13, 15, 16n, 17n, 91

Undecided voters, disposition of, 50–53

"Vanishing marginals," 16, 82. *See also* Incumbency
Vote/seat ratio, 2, 16, 82

Wolfinger, Raymond E., 14, 53
Wright, Gerald C., Jr., 22n

116